To Duane,

You are a fine Man,
and a good friend.
Peace and Blessings,
Denise Mellinger Slate

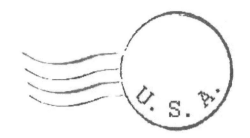

ODYSSEY

The Adventures of a

WWII Teenaged Sailor

by

Robert Bullard Perham

a.k.a. Jeremy Slate

as told to Denis Mellinger Slate

Odyssey: The Adventures of a WWII Teenaged Sailor

By Robert Bullard Perham, a.k.a. Jeremy Slate.
As told to Denise Mellinger Slate, 2001.

ISBN-13: 978-1542788540

Layout and print by Kevin Smith, Pixels Graphic Design,
Monterey, California.

Dedication

- - - - - - - - - - - - - - - - - - -

I originally began writing this story to give my family an opportunity to know more about me and my life before them. The results painted a wonderful picture of history. I realize how very lucky I have been throughout my many adventures. My life truly has been an Odyssey.

-Jeremy Slate

I dedicate this book to the thirty eight sailors, names unknown to me, who perished on the very same ship which carried me through my Naval adventure. And to all those heroic infantry men that fell onto the beaches of Europe. Peace.

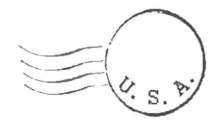

Chapter One

- -

The attack on Pearl Harbor did a lot of things to a lot of people. What it did generally though, was instill a pride in America born from that infamous day. Personally, it set me off on an incredible series of events.

It started like any Sunday on the farm. We'd milked the cows and I had the rest of the morning off; I was a chore boy on a dairy farm in Vermont. I had hired on a year before and expected to stay on until I graduated from High School down in Williamstown. Buster Brown from the next farm over had called me the night before, telling me that he could use my help in delivering some firewood the next morning. He knew that I would be off on Sunday morning, and it sounded like fun for a fifteen year old. Buster owned the only flat-bed Ford truck in the neighborhood and we loved riding on the back of it, trying not to slide off as we rounded corners a little too fast. I ambled on over.

December 7th 1941, was a cold sunless morning and a threat of an easy snowfall, or maybe rain. We set off on the back of the truck. I was accompanied by Buster's younger brother Henry, a year older than me. Our clothes were wet and we were cold to the bone when we arrived at the Judge's house with the load of wood. We warmed up by kicking the wood off the bed and onto the lawn. Then we really warmed up as we jumped down and stacked it. The Judge, an old man by now and well known, had run out of wood unexpectedly and we were doing him a favor. The whole operation took about as much time as it had taken to get over there, and we were soon on our way back to the Brown's.

Driving back, we sat in the middle of the bed, under the cabs rear window to keep warm. We had just rounded the corner and was headed up to the house, when both Henry and I heard it. It was a foreign sounding voice, as if it were coming from a long ways away. In this bucolic setting, the sound seemed eerily surreal before we figured it out that it was a voice from the radio. But what was the voice from the radio doing outside?

Buster must have heard it too, because he stepped on the brake, beginning the truck to a halt in front of the house. We stood up and looked over the cab. Someone had stuck the radio through the front porch window and it sat askew on the rocking chair...its wires extending back through the window. But that's not what caught our eyes. Grandfather Brown, up until then I don't think I had seen him outside of the house, was not only on the front porch...he was dancing!

He was tall and lanky and was doing some sort of jig, but wildly, as he kept yelling something. As soon as I

understood what he was shouting, a wave of heat passed
through my body.

"We're at war!!", he was shouting over and over while
clapping his hands to his jig. "We're at war!!"

The voice on the radio said something about Hickam
Field, that they were all running for cover and were being
shot at. I gripped the side of the truck, the heat was so
sudden. I recognized where it had come from. It was the
heat of inspiration. "We're at war!!", came again as
Grandpa danced on madly.

How could I feel inspired at a moment like this? Even
at the age of fifteen I knew war was bad. At the moment it
seemed to me that the past few years had gone by in
anticipation of something like this...an adventure.

Bob, Mom, and Pat at home in Margate, New Jersey.

Bob and Pat.

I am 11. My father snaps this picture
during a visit.

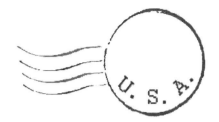

Chapter Two

- - - - - - - - - - - - - - - - - -

Until I was eight and my sister seven, everything was

all right. We lived in a beautiful house by the beach in

Margate, New Jersey. It was the house that I was born in on

February 17, 1926.

The back yard was the beach. Our father had left when I

was five, after a severe divorce in New York City. But we

quickly adjusted to life without him. In our house there

was three generations of females; my sister, our mother,

my mother's sister, and their mother, Nana. Life was

idyllic until we lost the house in the Depression and had

to split up. It was then, I believe, that my education as a

wanderer began.

Nana and Aunt Nat moved up to Rockville Centre near my Aunt Francis and Uncle Russ. My sister and I, with our mother, went east across the bay to Northfield, where we were given the upper floor in a rooming house, the owner being a friend of my mother's.

Removed from the ocean's edge, we felt unhappy in Northfield, but made the most of it. Our mother, meanwhile, had developed arthritis so severe that she became bedridden. My sister and I had plenty to do after that, making beds and getting groceries.

One sultry summer day we were advised that our father was going to pay us a visit. Although we feared our father, I'm sure that we both loved him. He was difficult for our minds to handle. We got our money and left for the Grand Union to buy some food for our fathers visit. On the way home, we saw his giant Packard Touring Sedan parked out in front of our house. The house was set back on the property and had a long path leading in from the sidewalk. As we passed the car and headed hastily up the path, we heard them.

They were shouting at each other, my mother's voice pleading and my father in his usual temper. We stopped at the bottom of the stairs, hearing them shout even louder. We ran to the side of the house and hid around the corner. Suddenly there was a pounding of feet on the stairs. The door slammed open and my father walked fast up the path. We were stunned to see our mother run out of the house after him, her black chiffon pajamas flapping behind her as she raced up the path, her voice pleading with him. It was the first time that we had seen our mother up, let alone running. When they were out on the sidewalk, we ran up to the hedge, and hiding behind it, watched as my father got in on the drivers side of his car and started it up. Our mother, meanwhile, had approached the car from the sidewalk and stood on the running board, leaning in towards my father. The convertible top was down so we could see the two of them and their confrontation clearly. Their voices were loud, echoing through the street. Suddenly his arm shot up and caught my mother. "Get off the car, Goddamn it!" were the last words we heard from my father as my mother, losing her balance backwards, fell onto the road, rolling several times, wrapped in her chiffon nightgown, as the car sped out of sight.

Their shouts had brought the attention of members of the firehouse next door, and as if waiting, the ambulance siren sounded almost immediately, picking up her lifeless form and driving away. We were left alone with our mother's friend, who also came out to watch.

My mother was in the hospital in Philadelphia for two months. We were not allowed to visit her. She had developed a rare skin disorder called Erysipelas, usually brought on by stress and often fatal. She died in October, at the age of forty two, our beautiful mother. Her name was Rebecca.

Almost immediately, we were returned to Margate and the home of Leath Cochran. She was my mother's closest friend, and in retrospect, I believe that they were lovers. Her house sat diagonally behind ours on the next block. The two back doors faced each other and were surprisingly close. We felt as much at home in her house as we did in ours. It felt odd that some other family lived in our house.

We stayed with Leath for two months. She visited Mother often and would return with uplifting news. Then one day, she returned visibly upset. She took us each by the hand and walked firmly up the stairs to our bedroom. By the time that we all sat down on the edge of the bed, she in the middle still holding our hands, we could tell she was trembling...the whole bed was trembling.

Looking straight ahead, she spoke for the first time. She whispered, "Your mother's gone." My sister almost immediately said, "Gone where?" I knew where she had gone. Leath answered, "Your mother's left you."

At this time she left us alone in the room. Neither one of us was crying, nor did we fully understand what had just taken place. My sister kept saying, "You mean we're never going to see mother again?" That idea struck me as inconceivable. We weren't taken to the funeral. So, the last time that we saw our mother, she was lying in the street.

My sister and I sitting in our beach backyard.
Margate, New Jersey.

Me and my sister with our grandmother
at her home in Margate, New Jersey.

The Browns.

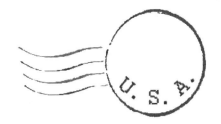

Chapter Three

_ _ _ _ _ _ _ _ _ _ _ _ _ _ _ _ _ _ -

Now we were the responsibility of my father who, at the time, had just landed a lucrative job at McGraw Hill Company. The Depression had ended for him. But he wanted none of the responsibilities of children. So he sent us to private school; my sister Pat went to a girl's school in Bristol, Tennessee and I found myself at the Peekskill Military Academy in upper New York, a beautiful sight overlooking the Hudson River.

The first two weeks were the strangest I'd spent this far in my short ten years. My mother had died a little over six months prior and here I was, alone with a bunch of strangers in a school with uniforms and hats and rifles and marching together on Sundays.

Those first weeks were spent listening to the quiet sobbing of my roommate, a twelve year old son of a Venezuelan Colonel in the Army. He was a sweet boy and would complain through sobs each night that he was so far from his home. His father would not be visiting him until Christmas and it seemed so far away. Listening to him, I tried to imagine, as I had so often lately, that I would never see my mother again. The words never and forever were much used in my thinking at the time. I was learning about infinity. It was not something that a ten year old boy should have to deal with.

I think that during the first weeks at Military School that I came to grips with the feeling of being on my own. After all, I was. My sister was in some far off school, and my father wouldn't be until Christmas. I was alone amongst strangers in a strange setting. I girded myself against all things and events and people. I was alone in this big world.

My first act was in a large study room, the first week, with every cadet present. Those in the fourth grade were asked to stand up and one by one, deliver their names. When that was done, they were asked to sit and those in the fifth grade were asked to stand. I had just come from the fourth in Rockville Centre. We'd been sent to Nana's apartment when our mother died. We lived there for a few months before being sent away by my father. I was in fourth grade, and at home received a great education from Nana. At the end of the school year I was amazed as the rest of the class when it was revealed by the teacher that I was one of two of the best students in the class.

Quickly taking all that into account, I remained seated when they called for the fifth grade students to stand. When they called for the sixth grade, I stood up and was duly counted among them without notice. I was thrilled. I learned to play the bugle and became the mascot of the football team, probably because I was one of the smallest in school. Of course, I attended every game. But my crowning achievement at Peekskill Military Academy was running away. I joined two older boys in a plan to flee from the Academy. It was pure gumption on my part; I'd loved the school up until then. I liked the uniforms and the organization of the marches on Sunday. I fell in love with Noxon, the polish that kept my bugle as shiny as my cap insignia and belt buckle.

I loved everything about the school, but took off purely for the adventure of having done it. We made it, too. Got as far as New Jersey before we were nabbed in a diner where we sat at the counter having ordered sandwiches. If I'd known that state troopers wore jodhpurs, I wouldn't have sat down next to one, but he asked us where we were from and the jig was up. It was a thrilling ride back to campus in a 1934 Ford convertible sedan, just what New Jersey state police were driving at the time.

My father had to pay an unexpected visit to the campus. We were all threatened with expulsion. But it was proved, at least for me, that there had been no bad feelings about the school, except perhaps, this was a way of letting off steam after so long being ritualized.

In any event, we weren't expelled, and from then on I acceded to the image of a pint sized icon on campus. You could say that was the imprint that made me an adventurer. After all, the rewards were far greater than I ever imagined them to be. Perhaps that was an element of adventure that only those who reach it find it.

And speaking of imprints, let me mention one that lasted no more than ten minutes, yet affected me enough to be considered important some sixty years later: One sunny morning we were all told to leave our classes and to form out on the great lawn overlooking the Hudson River. As we mustered out on the lawn, we looked up in the sky. The entire school was stunned into silence as slowly, majestically, the Hindenburg Zeppelin passed overhead at about ten thousand feet. This was the maiden flight.

It was an awesome sight. I remembered that it seemed like I could reach up and touch its sides. It wasn't until years later that I realized its size distorted my perspective. It was so huge and traveling at such a low speed that its propellers sounded like windmills, sort of gushing through the air, while the body of the deirigible took forever to pass us. I never forgot it and always have imagined what life would be like had that disastrous event never taken place, that terrible night when, on its second flight, it exploded.

Or was it that sunny day in 1931 when I was only five and with my sister, headed down to the ocean. Our mother had told us not to tarry too far, as we were to travel that day by train to Rockville Centre for a visit. But once we reached the water's edge, I borrowed an inner tube and sunk into it. I drifted off to sleep and woke up, badly sunburned, at least an hour later, out of sight of land. After much paddling and figuring out where the sun was going, I saw the silhouette of the boardwalk and the buildings behind it. A lifeguard, having patrolled the beach for several hours, looking out to sea with binoculars, spotted me and brought me to shore. I was four miles down the beach, in Ventnor, and it was seven hours later. I rode on his handlebars down to Douglas Avenue where we lived, but I caught my big toe in the spokes and he took me further down to the beach First Aid station, where he called my mother. When she found out that I wasn't really any the worse for the adventure, she lifted me up with a big smile of relief and a promise to heal the sunburn. I recall it as being a warm feeling of achievement, something I'm sure my mother didn't look at quite the same way.

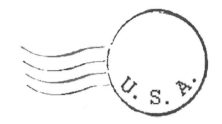

Chapter Four

- - - - - - - - - - - - - - - - - - -

At the end of the school year, my father, still chafing from having run off, commented as we sped south along the Hudson and stopped at Hastings-on-the-Hudson. Even though I wasn't expelled for my act, my father felt that I was having way to much fun and pulled me out. "Maybe these Nuns will beat some sense into you."

We drove through the iron gate and above it hung the iron words, "St. Clare's Academy". This June day was particularly humid, as we drove through lush woods and arrived at the top of the hill, upon which sat the school buildings.

To say the scene was a disappointment after Peekskill
Military Academy is a gross understatement. The Military
Academy stood on a proud promontory overlooking the
majestic Hudson River. The buildings had been of red brick
and had shiny white facades of columns and steps. These
buildings had no color to them at all. They were as gray as
the grass between them. I was to find that my sister would
also be attending this school. It was the only time that
Pat and I would attend the same private school. But it
didn't make any difference to us because the boy's school
and the girl's school were kept apart, in seperate
buildings even. So we seldom saw each other and then it was
just to surreptitiously wave at each other, like inmates
from another cell block. She was even required to wear a
uniform of pleated dark skirts and white blouses. We boys
were spared the code, but restricted nonetheless.

My sister didn't arrive at the school until classes had
begun in September. My father drove me down directly from

one school to another. I arrived at St. Clare's Academy just as summer vacation had started. During that summer, I was nearly alone in the school. There were three others that were to spend their vacations, not in school, but on the grounds of the Academy. It seemed ludicrous to describe this as an Academy after Peekskill Military Academy. But I was learning and I was learning fast; everything is not what it seems.

I lived that summer in a dormitory that, when school started, would sleep sixty two boys. It was a big, empty room filled with empty beds all summer long, with me and two others occupying the dormitory.

There were daily rituals which I'd have to carry out. I got used to a tablespoon of cod liver oil just before taking my cold shower with Fels Naptha soap. Those rituals stayed with me throughout the school session. Oh yes...Mass in the morning. It was known that I was not a Catholic, but I didn't mind the rituals...they were actually fascinating to me. I went to morning Mass often, dreaming that someday, if I behaved, I would wind up becoming an alter boy. That was something that I secretly wished for, although I couldn't take communion and I didn't have to confess each week. I wanted to confess. It seemed arcane and something to which I wanted to belong, but it was denied to me. Just as well.

What really made an impression upon me at St. Clare's were the woods. There were woods next to the property which extended several miles to Rice's dump at the far end. I became enamored of the woods. There had been no woods where I was raised, so close to the ocean. I made the woods my second home, getting out there every chance I got, which was quite often in the summer. I became a regular Tarzan, able to swing from tree to tree almost a mile before alighting. I was up there with the birds and snakes and other animals. I was observing them for the first time in my life. I watched tad poles become frogs, eggs become birds, and all kinds of insects. At the end, if I went that far, was Rice's dump, a fascinating place in its own way.

I remember that after school had started I continued to take hikes in the woods. I actually got a trap from somewhere and would leave it open in the woods overnight. The next day I would go out into the woods and find a black capped chickadee in my trap. I would study it for awhile and then let it go. But I had a close up view of what became for the rest of my life my favorite bird, the black capped chickadee. And salamanders, all kinds. It seemed that every time I turned over a rock there would be a different kind of lizard.

Rice's dump was a place where I learned a lot about how people live, and what they throw away. I found a lampshade, replete with some glass beads hanging from it as well as a rat that scurried out from under it while I collected its treasure. Later that year I made bracelets for Christmas presents. I used the glass beads and wire I had saved from the bottles of milk. I gave them to my grandmothers; Nana and Grandmother Perham.

But learning was what I was there for, and I learned a

lot...and learned it well. Much of what I learned during that year, I still remember. I remember as well as my late stays in the woods and the message delivered when I was late for supper. I'd come in from the cold and hold out my hands, palms down. A ruler was used to sharply remind me not to be late again. Sister Cherubim, the largest of the starched, black and white Nuns, had a particularly sharp way of delivering whacks.

I was very much a loner at St. Clare's. I had the military skills and now I was becoming a ranger. I read books, two a week, by Richard Halliburton. Books with titles like: The Royal Road to Romance and The Book of Marvels. They were all adventure books by a Princeton senior who went out and did things so he could say that he had done them. Like staying hidden during a visit to the Taj Mahal until all the visitors had left. Then, when the full moon rose in the night sky, he slowly and silently swam the distance of the rectangular pool up the middle of the Mosque. Or climbing the Matterhorn to spat for two thousand feet. He was accused while writing these popular stories, of fabricating most of them, but I didn't mind. My young mind was focused by then on adventure, and I thought of myself as a lone ranger riding through life on the wings of adventure, a wanderer and a taster of thrills.

By the time school was over, I wasn't yet an alter boy but I could recite the Rosary beads as fast as any Catholic. In fact, I didn't feel too bad because I already was observing how religion worked; you had to spend a lot of time in ritual, and I was already feeling that religion in my life would be a drag. So rather than embrace it after Mass every morning for a year, I came away a little afraid of the time I'd have to spend if I were, indeed, a religious person. I'd never heard anything about it from my family, except I knew that my mother was Episcopalian and my father didn't have any at all. From that moment on, religion played a negative role in my life and finally exited all together.

So I left St. Clare's and my father sent me to an upscale camp in the Adirondacks for the summer of 1938. I got a chance to play out my fantasies, living in a tent and paddling a canoe across the lake. It was a joyous summer, but now that I look back on it, I was preparing most of all to operate by myself.

I was accepting each challenge as an adventure and keeping by myself made the adventure so much richer. In short, I believe I was already figuring out that the adventure was the prime reason for being and the people that showed up in it were superficial to the experience. I was becoming self-centered.

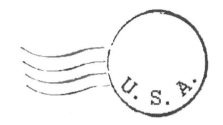

Chapter Five

- - - - - - - - - - - - - - - - - -

I had left Poke-O-Moonshine and was spending a week or two at my father's apartment with my sister. He had an apartment on the east end of 42nd Street in a raised little village, where the U.N. is now.

While we visited my father, the U.S. Navy sailed into the bay and up the Hudson River past the Statue of Liberty. My father gathered his mother from Greenwich Village, where she lived, and with my sister and me, took us to the McGraw Hill building where he worked. We went up to the thirty-second floor. From his office, we watched the fleet as it lay out in the River.

What was exciting to me was that my father had gone outside on a fire escape exit, and left us on the thirty-second floor expecting to return in a moment. Unfortunately the door closed behind him and he was locked out. He had to walk thirty-two flights down to the first floor before he could get out. Of course, my sister and I and our grandmother were wondering where he went, and were pretty paranoid when he showed up some hours later. He was quite winded but worried about us before he got a tongue lashing from his mother. His adventure stirred me more than the fleet.

My father had a strange sense of humor: He drove Pat and me almost to the iron gate at St. Clare's Academy before turning and heading toward Rye, New York, where unknown to us he had rented a house and had talked his mother into coming up and taking care of us. Of course, we were thrilled. In the first place we weren't going back to St. Clare's. Instead we were to try out something new, a home of our own in a nice town.

It so happened that Rye had a fantastic High School. (I recently attended the fiftieth reunion of my High School class and reconfirmed that the school was one of the best). I loved my year in Rye. We had a home and a family and I felt a part of it all. Pat was still in grade school and was down at Milton Point while I was up at Rye High in the eighth grade, the last grade of Junior High. I did well in school and easily drifted through. I had been primed by my education at St. Clare's and I was still reading. I spent most my time in the library, reading adventure stories by Lowell Thomas, Richard Halliburton and T.H. Lawrence; especially The Seven Pillars of Wisdom.

In September, before I was in school, we had a hurricane. The hurricane of 1938. I was down at the intersection below our house. It was flooded. I was in up to my chest, pushing cars through, when I realized that I was twelve years old and I would remember everything from that moment on. For one reason or another, that became the moment when I took responsibility for my own life and remembered all my thoughts after that.

Life in the suburbs was fine for my sister and me. Up to a point. The house had a built-in bar and the likes of a small tavern existed in our cellar. My father often had wild parties down there, with drunken acquaintances coming up from the cellar into my sister's bedroom, once vomiting on her bed while she tried to sleep

One afternoon after school, some local friends and I started cleaning up the tavern downstairs after a big party. There were half empty glasses at all the tables and I started drinking them up. By the time I went upstairs to supper, I was drunk. I didn't want to eat, couldn't, and excused myself as best I could, and went upstairs to my attic bedroom and collapsed. When I awoke, I was sitting on the edge of my bed with my father's fist coming at me. He punched me in the face, breaking my nose, and said, "So you were drunk, eh? How does it feel?" It felt bloody and my nose hurt and my father felt that I should never forget the first time. I never have.

Up to that time, sex hadn't played a part in my life. But all that changed one day in the library. Sitting opposite me was a girl that I had lent a nickel to for milk one day. Leaning over the table, she whispered, "I owe you a nickel. Do you want to take it out in trade?"

I had a job after school. There was a large Presbyterian church across the street from the High School. It had to be maintained in the winter months. I was given key to the back door. Each afternoon after school, I would run over to the church, let myself in, and first stoke the furnace. It was a coal burning stove and I'd scoop about four or five big shovels full of coal into the furnace. Then I'd walk through the church making sure that everything was as it should be.

So, that day in the library, when Cherry Day asked me if I wanted to take it out in trade, I don't know why or how, but I understood exactly what she meant. "Sure", I instantly responded. "Well, where and how?", she asked.

"Come around behind the church and knock on the back door after school", I said, suddenly enjoying the challenge. I don't think that at the age of twelve I was excited as much about sex as I was about the adventure.

I had just finished my last shovelful of coal and was stoking the furnace when I heard a loud knocking on the back door. Wiping as much coal as I could off my hands, I hastened to the back door and let Cherry in. We groped around the basement, with no lights and I entered one of the small storage rooms in the cellar. It was filled with extra pews, strewn around in an orderly fashion. Suddenly, Cherry had dropped out of sight. "Where are you?", I half whispered.

"Down here." She sounded deliberate, like where else would I be? I don't remember much after I followed her voice. I do know that we culminated the act. I don't remember what we said, if anything, and we were on our feet and stumbling over pews on our way out just as fast as we had communed.

It was growing dark in the winter light. I had my bike.
I offered to ride her home. She rode on my cross bar. I
remember thinking as we peddled through town, that everyone
who was looking at us knew what we had just done. In the
gathering darkness, I felt warmer than I usually did when
peddling my bike.

So I got that adventure out of the way at the age of
twelve. It would be a few years before sex would rear its
head at me, but I was happy that it was out of the way. I
felt that everything was going along just fine.

My grandmother by then denied my father a second
chance, stating that after this year she was going back to
Greenwich Village. Family life was too much for her. My
sister and I prevailed upon our father not to send us back
to St. Clare's and for once he tried to help us. He boarded
us out to a family not far from Rye High School.

The Sysak family was a good one and boarding with them

soon became fun because, among other things, the house didn't have a bar in the cellar, and it didn't have my father coming home and getting drunk. Instead, it consisted of two girls and a boy a little older than I. We got along well with all the family members and I recall that year with pleasure.

Boarding with the Syska's was a good experience. They let me build a darkroom in their cellar and I got into taking pictures. In the darkroom, I would develop the pictures and enlarge them. I also had a magazine route...Colliers...to deliver once a week. School zipped by in spite of some pretty heavy experiences. I was reading a book every week, all of them adventures; Lowell Thomas and all about the U boats in WWI, and my hero, Richard Halliburton, the Princeton gadabout. I particularly liked the story of how he was given more than twenty human heads as gifts from a tribe in Borneo. Later, flying through a storm in his open cockpit plane, he jettisoned the heads, one by one, to lessen the weight of his plane. That was the kind of adventure I sought in my dreams of aspiration.

Neither my sister nor I was surprised when, at the start of school, we were once again shipped off to private schools. My sister went to Ashburnham, Massachusetts to Cushing Academy, and I to Garden City, Long Island to St. Paul's School, an Episcopalian school of dynamic proportions. The facade of the main building ran uninterrupted for three city blocks. I don't know how many students were boarded there, but each of us had his own room. The main structure, three stories high, incorporated the rooms, the classrooms, the church, the mess hall, and a few other rooms. It was quite formal, more in line with the military academy than the rigors of Catholic school.

I became the smallest member on the football team, and did quite well academically. One day, I was one of six students caught doing what we weren't supposed to be doing in a place forbidden for us to enter, and I was off on another adventure. Toward the end of school, an upperclassman named Jack Comerford, a fellow football player, expressed concern for my future. He was from

Massachusetts, he explained, and was raised on a farm. "That's were you should spend the summer...on a farm!"

The idea appealed to me immediately. As soon as school was over and I found myself unwanted in my father's apartment in New York, I made up my mind. When my father said, "So what do you want to do this summer?" I replied, "I'd like to work on a farm." It got my father to laughing. He had a way of laughing at things I didn't expect. This was one of those times. I recognized it as more of a snear than a laugh. His response was to leave the apartment that morning and return, throwing a bus ticket to Bennington, Vermont and ten dollars on the bed. "There, that will get you to a farm."

My father at the time had teamed up with Sid Pike, the owner of the Skywriting Corporation of America. They were tight drinking buddies and had spent many weekends outside of Bennington in a small town called Pownal, where Sid had a lodge on the mountain. My father had taken my sister and me up there several times. We loved visiting Kenjockety, as it was called. My father and Sid would most often get drunk up there, but Pat and I found the countryside alluring and loved spending time up there.

So I took the bus to Bennington, unafraid and alone. Getting off the bus, I walked the nine miles back along the country road to the front boundary Kenjockety. I curled up in the woods beside the gate and went to sleep.

The postman, a friend of Sid's, came by in his truck. He picked me up, puzzled as to why I was there, then amazed as I told him the story. Chet Wadsworth then took me to his home in Bennington and his wife fed me. The next morning we went job hunting. He had a couple in mind and, just as he predicted, Lottie and Egbert Amadon took me on as their chore boy. Lottie and Egbert were in their sixties and both very active. He had a milking herd of forty one Holsteins and Gurnseys and a two hundred and fifty acre farm on the country road of East Pownal.

I loved working for them and had been there for a year

and a half, on that fateful day when we delivered a load of wood to the Judge and World War II had begun. Taking my background into consideration and allowing that I'd already had a full life and had only been around for fifteen years, and it was no wonder when I heard and saw Grandfather Brown dancing on the front porch, I felt the same inspiration warm my body. I was primed for another great adventure.

On the farm with Pat, Dad, Egbert, and Lottie Amadon.

Ruth McClain. She was my piano teacher.
I played in her father's square
dance band in High School.

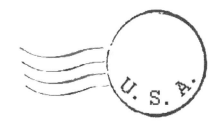

Chapter Six

- - - - - - - - - - - - - - - - - -

Always a wanderer, I found myself a year later working after school in a defense factory. I had left the farm and meandered south where I landed a job as a tractor driver on a large dairy farm in southern Williamstown. I boarded out with a family nearby. My new landlord was the manager at Sprague Electric Company in North Adams, just a few miles away. He got me a job at the plant.

Every day after school, I'd take the bus to North Adams and go to work. Because he was a manager, he was able to get me a special time segment, so when I went to work on the second floor, I was the only one at my end of the plant. Alone, I sat perched on a high stool where I tested electrical resistors. The resistors, different sizes for different wattage, looked like a firecracker with a fuse (or wire) at each end. I had a set of runners in front of me which carried electricity decided by me.

When testing the resistors, I would hold it by its body and run it towards me, making sure that each end of the firecracker ran across my runners, making electrical contact. All the while leaning back from the table because I had a box of resistors in my lap. I'd run each resistor towards me and when one of them burned out or didn't make contact, I'd discard them.

Once, while testing a firecracker at seven hundred and fifty volts, my chair slipped out from under me, forcing me forward against the table. My left forearm came down across the two runners and I was thrown backwards by the jolt. It took me awhile to recover and I had two welts across my forearm as a souvenir of the most electricity I'd ever absorbed.

But being alone in that part of the plant for eight hours after school had its benefits. There was a public address system over which the latest songs were played. I remember "Woodchoppper's Ball" by Woody Herman, among others. But the greatest hit of all came out in November, and for a month, until I left the plant and headed south, I was enraptured that winter by the strains of "White Christmas" by Bing Crosby. Every time I hear that song, after all these years, I'm taken back to that Defense plant in North Adams.

I wouldn't be seventeen until February, but the thought of joining up was already in my mind, as it was with so many young men of the time. I knew I could join at seventeen, legally if I had one of my parent's signature. Being a wanderer, I didn't plan ahead much but it seemed as if I had a plan from then on. That plan was...to get me into the service as quick as possible.

My father wanted me off the farm. I told him that I

would return to Rye, where I had a room on the third floor of an old Victorian. Also, with a room on the third floor, was Eddie Clay. Eddie was a well known student at Rye High because he was a great trombone player. Eddie and I soon became good friends. I learned from Eddie to go to sleep with the radio on. He'd go to sleep listening to Art Ford and the Milkman's Matinees program on WNEW. I've had that habit ever since and my last words to Eddie, who when dying of lung cancer years later at Port Chester, was that every time I go to sleep with the radio on, which is very often, I think of the good times we had in life. He got that infectious grin on his face, in spite of the tubes, and I left him just like that. He died the next morning. But I'd told him.

I never make plans for the future. A wanderer, by his very nature, cannot do that. So I don't remember Eddie and me making plans about enlisting. But we must have been discussing it. So on the sixteenth of February, just a day short of my seventeenth birthday, we acted as if we had a plan. But this is all that I can recall: At around ten in the morning of a cold, dreary day we met in the bathroom or someplace with Tommy Black and Ralph Blohm, classmates of ours. At ten thirty that morning the four of us left school and started hitch hiking into New York, some eighteen miles to the south. I remember that we broke up, two apiece, on the trip down but somehow all met in the city and got down to 20 Church Street, where we were to enlist.

Ralph Blohm and Tommy Black decided for the Army. Eddie Clay went for the Marines. I, in the tradition of my father, my favorite cousins Russell and Jack Phillips, and their uncle Jack Phillips. Uncle Jack had been a hero at Pearl Harbor, sailing his ship the U.S.S. Neosho, a tanker that was free of port, saving the ship and its crew. Rear Admiral Jack Phillips was awarded the Navy Cross.

I knew that my father had been in the Navy. But since then, I've learned that he served for a year and a half and managed to go overseas to Ireland, where he was involved with the young and burgeoning Navy Air Force. So I went for the Navy. Of course, when they learned of my age, at first refused to give me a physical. But when I told them that I would be seventeen the next day and that my father was willing to sign, they let me through. They told me that they wouldn't send for me until sometime afterwards. Since we had all determined to go that day, it came as a disappointment to me. But when I found out that none of the other three were going that day, I wasn't so disappointed.

Tommy Black had been accepted in the Army. But Ralph Blohm had been rejected...poor eyesight...and from that day on, Ralph was known as "Rabbit" Blohm. Every day after the exam he'd show up at school, munching on a carrot. He did this until June when he graduated. Ralph did eventually get into the Army and was killed in a glider landing at Normandy. Tommy Black was killed at Iwojima. Eddie Clay was accepted into the Marines, but like me, he was told that he would be called up later.

Early in March, I received a notice stating that I'd be called in on the 19th of March. Eddie Clay would have to wait until graduation, just three months away. The night before I was inducted, I lay in my bed, too excited to sleep, pondering my next adventure. The next morning I returned to Church Street. I, along with several hundred others, each held some sort of bag, our last connection to civilian life.

I don't remember what sort of train we were on. It was to take us to Chicago, where we were to transfer to a train that would take us to Great Lakes Naval Training Station on Lake Michigan in Illinois. There were several hundred of us so I imagine that we occupied only part of the train. It was not a troop train.

Almost everyone of us was drafted. Very few, me among them, had enlisted on their own. This was brought to my attention by one who was drafted. His name was Larry Storch. He was a funny man, and I was intrigued with him. He told me he was heading for show biz, albeit a strange route, and would make the most of his experience in the Navy to better himself along those lines. It wasn't long before he'd been transferred to entertainment and went on to fame within the Navy. He was a brilliant observer and imitator. (Years later, after I'd been in show biz myself, and while I was appearing in "Look Homeward Angel", he was on Broadway in, I think, "Flower Drum Song". Anyway, I went to see his performance. I went backstage afterward and introduced myself. Disappointingly, he didn't remember anything about our relationship, seeming to recall something on the train, but unsure even of that. I was heart broken. But that's show biz!

I was doing okay in boot camp when I came down with pneumonia. I had played the trumpet in the school's music class so I volunteered as bugler in boot camp. I was given reveille, which had me getting up at four thirty, instead of five, and blasting away with the bugle come rain or shine. I got pneumonia and was pretty close to death. I developed pleurisy so fast and I distinctly remember hearing the following conversation at the foot of my bed. "Should we call his father?" "Where does he live?"...... "New York." After a lengthy pause, "No, he wouldn't get here on time anyway." I rallied after hearing that and here I am today, some dozen or so bouts with pneumonia, the latest being a week ago, because of weak lungs. But ironically, I had huge lungs..."the lungs of a Bolivian Indian" so described a Peruvian doctor upon looking at my lengthy lungs for the first time. But they were weak, which led to my becoming, officially, a disabled veteran with a ten percent disability.

I survived boot camp although it took me longer to get out than the others. I was interviewed for job possibilities after boot camp. What had I done productively in my short seventeen years? Well I was a tractor driver, skilled in all kinds of farm equipment, and, oh yes, I worked in a defense plant for three months. "Doing what?" I was asked. I was testing electrical resistors. "Now we're getting somewhere. You studied electricity?" Well...not quite. "We'll make you an electrician!" Just like that.

I was sent to the "other side" as we called the separation between boot camp and schools of further study, like electricity and machine shop. As I recall, boot camp was on the inside of the train tracks while the "graduate" schools were on the side of the lake. So we didn't even see the lake in boot camp.

I made a big connection when I started my first class. A family connection. The first text from which we learned about electricity was written by the "wireless wizard of WWI", a rear Admiral in the Navy whose name was William Hannum Grub Bullard. My grandfather on my mother's side, who died three years before I was born, was named Ellsworth Flagg Bullard. He and the Rear Admiral were brothers. I was mighty glad at that point that I'd chosen the Navy.

It might have been that such pride in learning from that book, but whatever it was, I learned a lot. I still know about electricity probably more than you know. That attitude sticks with me because I think that electricity got a bum rap when the internal combustion machine was invented and all that dirty oil started coming to the surface, where it didn't belong...that's why it was down there in the first place.

But think of it. What if Thomas Alva Edison beat out John D. Rockefeller in his bid for power? I'll bet that everyone in the U.S.A. Would know what a volt is and what an ampere is and what wattage is, just for starters. We'd be further along toward cold fusion or some other means of arriving at electricity. We are still in the stage of storage batteries, the creation of electricity from a chemical reaction. If we could just spend as much money and time on research and development toward electricity as we do on petroleum and all its by-products. You must realize that the plastics industry as such would be non-existent. Think about life without plastics. Think of such simple things as cellophane. I mean it.

If Thomas Alva Edison had won as big a battle as John D. Rockefeller, just think of what society would be like. The internal combustion machine, for instance, would be non-existent. When was the last time you spent a day without the sounds of internal combustion machines. Just think about that world...then learn about electricity.

On a visit to Kenjockety.

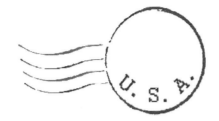

Chapter Seven

- - - - - - - - - - - - - - - - - - -

On one afternoon of many I'm sure, I found myself with several friends from class standing at a corner juice bar, where we often bought Cokes or sassafras, or birch carbonated drinks of the time. When asked what I wanted, I answered, I think I'll have a Coke please", at which a petty officer standing behind me was clearly overheard to jive my delivery. He accented the word please to sound quite effeminate.

That day, in the context of where I was, I inwardly panicked, because I thought I was revealing something of my nature that was absolutely forbidden, my sexual orientation, which at the time was totally inhibited. I felt that many of my true feelings were indeed weird, and that no one else, particularly the Navy, should ever become suspicious. That feeling of terror never again entered my mind, even though, as a true sailor, what I did on my shore leave or liberty was my own business.

The next weekend was my first liberty since entering the Navy some three months prior. It was a weekend pass and I had a choice of either Chicago or Milwaukee. Oddly enough I chose Milwaukee. As soon as I arrived I went shopping for a tattoo artist. I had learned of several and finally chose one. I got one so that there would be no question as to where I was coming from. It was a clipper ship at full sail through a red sunrise, with four seagulls in the sky. Under the ship, within a scroll that spread across the bottom, were the capitalized letters U.S.N. Now I thought, as soon as I get my ship I'm going to go out and buy me a dress uniform of gabardine and bell bottoms.

I went to a bar and met a girl. We went to her place, a

small farm on the outskirts of the city. She took me by the hand into the garage and lay down over a bale of hay. I easily recalled how, and was just getting busy, when suddenly it sounded as if it were raining, right there in the garage. I instantly stopped what I was doing, and scared to death I said, "What was that?" "Rabbit raisins!" she said sharply, leaving no room to ask another question. I spent the next couple of minutes figuring out that we were lying across a rabbit hutch. By the time I'd figured that out all else had ended...and my tattoo hurt.

On my next liberty to Milwaukee I joined a gang of rowdy sailors and we got rooms for a buck a piece at a hotel in downtown Milwaukee. Jan Garber's Orchestra was playing on the roof. I didn't go up. Instead, we rowdy's got a whole bunch of condoms, filling them with water and sent bombs away down seventeen floors before I decided that might be dangerous, and quit. But I didn't go up to listen to Jan Garber. Instead, I met up with another girl and she also took me home.

Now, instead of leading me into a darkened house, she took me to the cellar and opened the doors. She told me in whispers that at the bottom of the stairs was the kitchen to the house. As she closed the doors above us, she instructed me to sit on the stairs. Instinctively, I dropped my pants and she lifted her skirt before she sat down on my lap. Suddenly and without warning, the kitchen light came on, exposing her mother's back at the ice box. In a panic we sat there, she securely on my lap, unable to move, and watched as her night gowned mother sleepily turned out the lights and went back upstairs. I'm surprised that we weren't terminally frozen in that spot. We sat without moving or talking forever, it seemed, before she lifted off my useless lap and opened the cellar doors.

When I returned to the hotel, Jan Garber was still playing upstairs. I wasn't enthused, so I went to bed. I remember thinking that if the girls mother hadn't interrupted us, and if Benny Goodman was playing upstairs, then it would have been a perfect night.

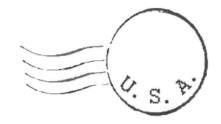

Chapter Eight

- - - - - - - - - - - - - - - - - - -

After graduating from electricians school, I was sent to a secondary course in New York City. I was to study electricity at the Hell's Gate Power Station of the Manhattan power project. I became a resident of Pier 92 for the next three months.

I learned a lot in those three months, attending school five nights a week. I became the shadow of the man in charge, following behind him as he threw switches, brought huge generators on line, worked with shunts four feet long and as wide as your fist. All this under the roar of the

East River as it coursed through the Hell's Gate power station.

The other thing I learned, the thing that proved invaluable view of some day getting aboard a ship, was where I lived. Pier 92 was a famous Cunard Line Pier. It docked the Queen Mary. (Alongside that, on Pier 94 lay the French liner Ile de France on its side, having been scuttled by unknown forces. Sadly it lay there throughout the duration of the war.) During the war, transatlantic travel for tourists stopped and the Mary was put into service transporting troops.

Pier 92 was at least a quarter of a mile long and barely two hundred feet wide. It was stripped of the customs area, the baggage area and the various sundry items necessary for boarding about two thousand passengers on any given day. In its stead, lined up in rows of a dozen or so, were triple decker bunks, welded to the deck. Rows and rows. You had to be real careful to recognize your bunk, as you could get lost and therefore spend a long, long time trying to find it. Usually, a few thousand sailors would be milling about, compounding the maelstrom. I was one of a very few that had come there for schooling. Pier 92 was best known as a recovery pier; the place where survivors of Atlantic sinkings were brought, often in the oil soaked condition that they were found floating in. You could always identify the most recent survivors in the mess line. They'd have a certain glazed look on their faces and their hair was always messed up. They looked like they had just come in from a freezing soaking.

I would return from school at dawn and saw many survivors pulling in from the dark sea. They were discharged and told to find an empty bunk. Of course, they'd have nothing with them but the clothes on their backs. You'd think that we were losing the war the way they kept coming in, from tankers mostly. They were Maritime sailors with no real uniforms, and plenty of them. I particularly liked it when survivors of a fighting ship were brought in. Especially the Destroyers. The very word suggested a sworn duty of the sailors on board. They seemed different from the rest.

Accustomed might be a good word to describe their behavior. Most of the Destroyer men acted as if they were accustomed to it, as if they'd been in other sinkings. These sailors were special and they showed it. Their well known walk was more of a swagger that developed after they had been subjected to everything the ocean could deliver, and still walked the decks. That swagger was not one born of hubris. It was a necessity for standing upright on a ship. These ships, rather than sailing, cut through huge waves like a knife, three hundred and forty-eight feet in length and only thirty-six feet wide. I knew the dimensions of a Destroyer before my tenure was up on Pier 92.

All that hustle and bustle on a pier made famous for its gentlemanly behavior among the wealthy, was now receiving on a daily basis, all the men, with oil glazed looks on their faces.

I learned a lot of lore on Pier 92. I spoke fluent

seamanship, and my eyes were opened to earrings, unheard of in those days, but as unarguable then as a football hero wearing one today. Usually they has a hanging star and it seemed always to be on the left ear only. And dress...Destroyer sailors wore bell bottoms, invented in the Navy for easily swabbing decks. These bell bottoms were not Government issued (GI) but had to be privately purchased. They were forbidden to be worn, except when the sailors were at sea.

It seemed that there was just enough, one hundred and twenty five men on board, for one to know all, and it made for a pretty tight ship. In view of the fact that below decks the bunks were lined up three high against a wall which was so thin, the Destroyer sailors used to refer to their ships as "tin cans" because between their sleeping bodies and the roaring ocean was only five-eighths of an inch of steel. Below decks, you could indeed hear the roaring of the ocean. When I had the opportunity to roll up my sleeves and reveal my tattoo, the Destroyer sailors it seemed were more aware of it, telling me it was a good one.

My schooling ended before the Navy had made plans for me. I was thrilled to find out that I would be transferred to the Norfolk Training Station, Norfolk, Virginia. I was thrilled because it was known as a Destroyer base. Maybe I would luck out. It seems that I always did.

After Pier 92, Norfolk was a quiet dream. I was introduced to the Quonset hut, home for fourteen soldiers...and a shower. One of the things that I can recall about that stay was my first purchase of a ball point pen, I think it was a Reynolds, at the PX..and Vanilla ice cream. I must have been trying to put on some weight because I got in the habit of every night going down to the PX and buying a quart of Vanilla ice cream. I'd take it back to the hut, eat it all, and then take a shower. That was pretty much the routine I remember, and not much else.

I wasn't there too long. Christmas was on its way. It had been just a year after I'd heard"White Christmas" at the defense plant. Now here I was all the way down in Virginia. I hitch-hiked home for Christmas. I got in a horrendous accident in New Jersey when my driver, a real drunk with an attitude, didn't see a toll station and tried to drive right through the station. He nearly killed the ticket dispenser. He was carried off raving mad. All this to the strains of this year's Christmas hit, Perry Como singing "I'll Be Home For Christmas". Toward the end of my trip, I was singing that song in earnest. I hitch-hiked on the Long Island and found myself home at the Phillips house, a hero in a Navy uniform. I missed Russell and Jack as they were off fighting the war.

It took me less then a month after returning to Norfolk to be assigned...and it was a Destroyer!! What a ship! Its name was the U.S.S. Murphy and it already was rumored to have a giant, green shamrock pasted up on the after stack. The word nomenclature comes to mind at this point.

While nomenclature is described as a general term used to identify a particular set or system, the word as used in the Navy refers to that "different language" on board a ship. From now on, as I get closer to actually boarding my ship for the first time, I'll probably slip into nomenclature.

In the Navy, ships are classified by tonnage. Thus, the Murphy was of the30's class. One thousand six hundred tons isn't a small ship, you say. It is when it is compared to a battleship at 72,000 tons! There were different styles of Destroyers. There were still some four stackers left over from World War I that saw service. They had the classic, traditional look. Their profile was definitely World War I. But the Murphy had stacks that were raked and flat sided, to give it a 1937 modern design. In the Navy it was called "a slab stacked broken deck class". It started high out of the water at the bow, came back through the pilot house, and just behind the pilot house the deck took a turn downward one full deck. It gave the Murphy a distinct look.

How did I know all this without having seen the ship yet? Jane's, that's how. There's a tome of war planes, ships, et all of practically every nation compiled in picture form by Jane's, a British publishing company. We used them extensively for identification of planes. Needless to say, I was excited.

As the hour approached, I found out more about my ship. Some months before, the Murphy and several other Destroyers escorting a convoy of merchant ships and tankers to England. Leaving the port of New York just before dark, they were a hundred and fifty miles off the coast when turning, signals somehow got mixed up. A tanker cut hard right at the same time the Murphy cut left. The tanker hit the Murphy just aft of the pilot house about two in the morning of a full moon. The bow capsized and sank almost immediately, taking thirty eight men to their deaths. The Murphy, or part of it, was towed back to New York backwards, receiving a hero's welcome as she was towed up the East River to the Brooklyn Navy Yard. They had put a new front end on the ship and she was getting ready for her shakedown cruise.

I can't remember how I got up there. All I remember is walking into the Brooklyn Navy Yard in the middle of a cold, cold night, with all the lights blazing. It sounded like every machine was running. The huge cranes were moving up and down their tracks. There were shouts, clangs, bells ringing, and it was one in the morning. They were building a battleship, the U.S.S. Missouri, right there in a huge dry dock alongside my ship. I had my pea coat up tight around my neck. It was bone chilling cold amid all that steel. Even the smell of diesel oil was muted. I walked up to the dock and stood there, suddenly warm while seeing through my breath, the ship...my ship...for the first time. I never even thought of the war. This was going to be my home for the next years. I was going on board, and once there, would never again see the shore as I was used to seeing it. I was going to sea. At this moment, that was enough for me. I threw my sea bag over my shoulder and stepped toward the gangplank. I was about to embark on adventures beyond even my imagination. And this ship would take me there. That was the night of January 16, 1944. I was still seventeen, for another month. I lifted my free arm up to a salute. I said, "permission to come aboard, sir." "Permission granted" was all that I needed to hear.

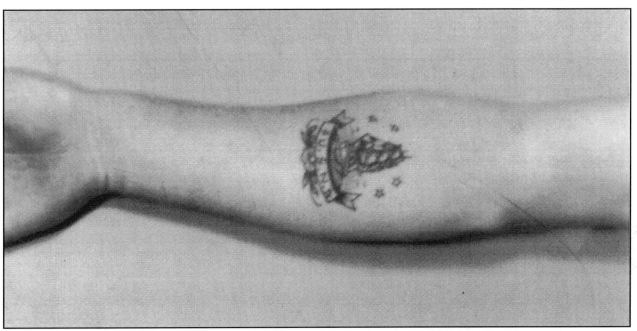

My tattoo before having it removed.

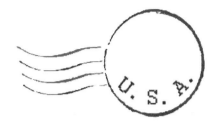

Chapter Nine

- - - - - - - - - - - - - - - - - - -

I was a third class seaman striking for electrician's mate. The third class seaman was the lowest rank in the Navy. It didn't take long to become second and then first class seaman. I don't even remember how it went, but I know that I was a first class seaman before we got underway.

I was given a bunk on the port side aft, where everyone from striker's to machinist's mate, electricians mate, and every job that required duty below decks wore his rank on the left sleeve, while Bos'n's mates, Quartermaster's and every rank that dealt with duty above decks wore his insignia on the right sleeve. They slept forward of the pilot house, in the bow of the ship.

There were about 115 of us, all told, on board. Since I was new to the crew, I was given a bunk against the bulkhead and I soon learned maneuvers that avoided my shoulder from striking the bunk above me when I rolled over. Actually, one of the first things that I learned on board was to keep your head out of the way. It was astonishing how often I struck my head in a day. And you learned never to run too fast up or down the ladder. Oh yes, you also learned, thanks to nomenclature, that there are no stairs aboard a ship. They are all ladders. Ladders behavior was specific...the lower ranked person was always the first going down and the last going up. In the event of a slip or fall, the lower rank would be there to catch the victim. There were practical reasons behind almost every bit of nomenclature. There were actual ladders on board. They were all under the hatch covers. Once a hatch was removed, access down into the ship was straight, the ladder extending down into the hold. There were escape hatches all over the ship. Each compartment below deck had one.

From the bow backwards, the ship looked like this: Most of the above deck crew was housed up there. Bunks through the ship were three high. There were bunks up against the bulkhead and there were bunks standing in the middle. The ones on the side, like mine, were capable of being lifted and hinged up to the bulkhead to allow more passage space down below. But most of the time it was ignored and didn't make any difference. I'm sure the 114 other members on board felt the same way that I did.

Many years later, while living in Manhattan and having to walk to work, I made the same rule that I kept aboard ship; no matter how fast that you travel, never touch another person. You'd be amazed at what a great game that could be. All of us seam to practice it. I don't remember every bumping into someone. The only time that I actually collided with another crew member unintentionally, was when I was standing behind Bill Snow during battle stations and he was thrown back into me, but that was understandable...

and a bump I'll never forget. He had used his wet fingers to quickly locate a blown fuse on the control board. He indeed found the troubled spot, which sent a blast of electricity through him, knocking him back onto me.

We were trained to sort of slither around. You soon found out that your hands, while walking, kept quite busy. You were always reaching out for the next thing to grab, be it a rung on a ladder or just walking down the deck, holding onto the lifeline stretched from one end to the other. You're always prepared to be thrown on a Destroyer. The last place you want to be thrown is overboard. I learned all this before ever establishing a set of sea legs.

On the deck above the bow, were two gun mounts and from them protruded the barrels of five inch guns, actually the smallest gun in the Navy. A Battleship's guns, in comparison, are sixteen inches. Some people referred to the five-inchers as "rifles". But they were extremely accurate at short range. The second gun back set higher than the first. In that space under the bow, there were also the food supplies. This was in the days before Birdseye, so we had a huge walk-in refrigerator. It was situated close to the ship's dining area, directly under the pilot house and just forward of the break in the deck. The mess line started down the deck on either side, and when it reached the ladder at the break in the deck, went down instead of up, leading directly into the mess hall, or galley. Situated somewhere above the galley in that general area, were the Captain's and the Executive officers quarters. Also the warrant officer, the gunnery office and all the other ranks. We had two chief petty officers on board. One above, and one below. Our chief petty officer had been an electrician's mate, so he would turn out to be partial toward any and all who occupied the electrician's shack.

On the top deck aft of the mess hall, were the various shops which kept the ship running; the machinist's shop, by far occupying the largest space, the laundry, which was permanently manned by two crew members working all the time. The radio shack was located back by the galley, and the electrician's shop was aft of the machinist's shop, the last shop along that part of the ship. Above the shops were the two raked stacks and between those were the torpedo tubes, five of them alongside each other. There was a break in the superstructure aft of the electrician's shop, then another group above deck, including the latrine and the steps to the after bunks which typically belonged to those whose job was below decks and who wore their insignia on the left arm. We were all bunched up and classified under one name, something like "the bilge rats".

Above the after superstructure was a third gun and its mount. Just aft of that superstructure was the fantail, or stern of the ship, upon which sat a fourth five-inch gun. It was generally clear with a hatch situated just above the rudders of the ship and its two screws each weighing 45 tons and capable of making this a 348 foot speed boat, able to do 37 knots or about 40 miles per hour. Off to the side of the stern were the ash cans, or depth charges that were to be rolled off the stern when intercepting U boats. On either side of the ship, slightly astern, were two davits, each holding a twenty-six foot whaleboat with a diesel engine.

Just over the electrician's shop was a giant thirty-six inch searchlight. It didn't take long to figure out that I was scared to death of being shocked. Ever since the experience at Sprague Electric. I even got nervous screwing in a light bulb. So the chief gave me the job on board of making sure all the batteries were up to date.

There were quite a few backups on board. Each gun, each vital section of the ship, was electrically backed up by batteries. I was kept busy all day maintaining them, wearing out a pair of jeans every week. The acid even got my shoes after a while. My battle station was the thirty-six inch light. But when they weren't using the light, I was assigned the twenty millimeter machine gun on the port side, up by the torpedoes between the stacks. My station while underway was the after steering room, back in the fantail. We also had two engine rooms and two boiler rooms, which were called fire rooms. There was a section of the engine room that was the power board for the two generators

I almost wrecked the ship before it left the harbor; Bill Snow had taken a liking toward me and since he was in charge of the big electric board, he let me hover over him, learning how the board works. Putting the generators on line and putting one up to speed and connecting it to the other generator was the usual practice. Bill showed me on the panel that when the arrow pointed upright, at twelve o'clock, to pull the switch that would put my generator on line with the second generator, which was already up to speed.

It was about ten in the morning. We were to get both generators up and running for a test. Bill let me throw the switch. I stood there, waited until the meter was one hundred and eighty degrees out of synch with the second, and pulled the switch. I heard Bill mutter, "Oh no!" under his breath just as the entire ship, in one giant thump, lifted itself out of the water. When it came down, everything electrical on board had stopped. The engine room was filled with dust from the shaking. What I had done was to kick my generator in at precisely the wrong time; the equivalent of smashing two generators, each weighing several tons, into each other at breakneck speed. I had suffered a clear case of dangerous dyslexia, but long before the word was even invented. On top of being embarrassed, I was scared out of my wits. The word "court marshal" immediately came to mind.

I was called up to the Exec's office. Mr. Klee must have taken mercy on my poor, scared soul. Along with Bill's support, I managed to stay aboard, never to touch that switch again. Actually, it was shortly after that incident that I was put in charge of the storage batteries.

I had been aboard about a month when the word came. We were to leave port and try her out for a day. We'd been newly painted and you couldn't see where the new started from the old. It looked perfect. But with a vessel this size, a quarter inch off could mean a different setting. Everything needed to be checked out. Before we were to go on our shakedown cruise, the skipper wanted to know just how she would behave.

Once we were out in the river, things went pretty smoothly. But it was getting underway that was exciting. For the first time, I heard the Bos'n's whistle over the PA system and the pronouncement, "Station special sea detail. Prepare to get under way." By now I'd been somewhat of an enigma in the electrician's shop; I'd committed what was to date the most grievous crime a seaman third class striking for electrician's mate could have committed, yet I seemed to be the special pet to the chief of the shop, Bill Snow. Perhaps that he felt guilty for giving me so much responsibility so soon after I'd come aboard.

We separated the ship into sections and then established crews for each one. Bill Snow always had me in his crew. There were usually three or four in a crew. But we had muster. The whistle. Then, "all hands on deck." Everyone went topside and got in line. Our Executive officer, one down from the Captain, name of Bill Klee, was terse and to the point. "This is a historic moment for the

Murphy. But more important today, is the Brooklyn Navy Yard, for we are going to find out if what they've done is working. And if it all works, we're on our way", he said.

There were uncontrolled huzzahs from several in line. Most of them were veterans from Sicily, where the ship had been before. They remembered the thirty eight men who went down with this ship, or at least part of it. They remembered Sicily, when a five-inch shell burst through the port side, beheading the man standing in front of the board. Ferguson and Jacobsen had both been down there. Now we were stationing special sea detail with a ship of memories and one of the future, at least the bow faced the future. We were about to find out how compatible the past was with the new future.

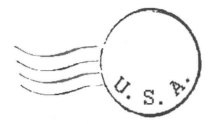

Chapter Ten

- - - - - - - - - - - - - - - - - -

My station by then was in the after steering room, the room at the very tail of the ship, under the hatch, that raised hatch; it often got wet back there and you didn't want any water pouring down into the steering engine room. The steering engine room was, to me, my secret stronghold on the ship. Like the job in the defense plant, I was alone on the job back there. It was a small space, occupied mainly by the tops of the two giant rudders that extended beneath the ship. My station was directly under the hatch, which had me facing the back of the ship. In front of me was the gyro compass and the steering wheel; the wheel was the same style as they used up forward in the pilot house. The same size, solid with a rubberized handle.

The purpose of the compass and the steering wheel was if the pilot house were cut off in battle, I'd be responsible for getting us out of trouble. I would take over, manually if necessary, steering the ship, indeed while we were underway. I had to get used to the realization that every command, every feeling I had, was reversed. I was facing aft while steering the ship forward! It was a fascinating watch. I came to love it. I'd put on the headset which kept me in touch with the pilot house, sit perched up on the hatch opening, sailing along on a dark sea, watching the mast of the ship rise and fall in the darkness. But all that lay ahead.

What I watched now, from my hatch back aft, the sight of lines being tossed on board from the shore gave me a thrill just watching. The ship shuddered slightly as it moved away from the dock and slowly eased out into the East River.

I had to get used to the whole ship shuddering. Of course it shuddered; it had the strength of 450,000 horses, why not shudder? She was actually holding back, like a great steed, from asserting itself. I felt like I was along for the ride, a feeling of authenticity, that's how much I had to do on this first cruise. I let the ship introduce itself to all its crew members. It was a good intro as we sailed up the East River toward Long Island Sound. Mostly we were cruising, sort of floating down the river.

Automobiles stopped along the East River Drive or slowed down and honked their horns. Some children even carried flags and waved them at us. This wasn't an unique experience for most people walking the East River. About every other day, it seemed, a ship would back out of the Brooklyn Navy Yard and cruise up the river just as we were. But it was a thrilling sight, nonetheless, and as we approached a wide part of the river, started to turn about.

For some reason, the one thing that stands out in my

memory of that day, was the turning around. It wasn't so much the actual maneuver as it was its consequences. As the ship turned, it sort of slid around, and the surface of the water became a bright sheen for several hundred yards. The surface became like a mirror. This happened each time we maneuvered from side to side going up the river.

We tied up in the same spot in the yard. The ship had responded to commands as if she had always been one with herself. Everyone was mighty pleased with the way everything had gone.

Now came the finishing touches. Next stop, according to Mr. Klee, was Casco Bay, Maine, where we would go for our shakedown. I don't think anyone, even the vets, had their sights on anything but getting into the shakedown cruise. We weren't thinking about where we were going. We weren't even thinking about the war. We were concentrating on making this ship seaworthy and that was that. I seemed to be getting along with everyone even if I was known as "that kid that lifted the ship out of the water". The crew gradually melded into one, but those who were new were always reminded of the 38 who died. That was the only visible difference between the new members and the old. The old members, like Ferguson and Jacobsen accepted us, the new ones who were anxious to get under way, like Rachon and LeBlanc and Charlie Potoroff and Joe Buck, the half Indian electrician. I remember Joe Buck was a great kid and always had something humorous to say about any event. f

When the moment came that the new ship would get underway, the crew were together as one. The veteran crew had been generous toward us and it paid off. We were a fighting unit, that much we knew.

The skipper came over the PA to tell us that we were ready. It was the Captain himself who gave the order, "station special sea detail", which meant that in twenty minutes we would be ready to cast off. Our skipper was also among the new on board. He was usually a soft spoken person who resembled more than an officer in the Navy...a president of a bank, and by gosh, that's what he was in civilian life.

Royal Wolverton had come from a bank in the center of the country, like Witchita, Kansas, or some place like that. In the next two years he would prove to be a competent sailor, guiding the Murphy through the war with hardly a scratch. I don't know where other officers came from in civilian life. William Klee, our Executive officer, was direct and concise. He was perfect for his title. There was a great big, kid like appearance about the gunnery officer whose name I don't remember.

Mr. Soloman was close to the enlisted men because his rank, that of warrant officer, was one step up from their side...the petty officer. Soloman had been a chief petty officer and actually was the only rank that was awarded to an enlisted man, making him a commissioned officer in the step up. He was the liaison between those who enjoyed the privilege of special meals and special quarters, waited on by black seamen, who could only hold jobs in the galley. Prejudice was something still strange to those of us who'd grown up in segregated conditions. We took certain things for granted.

The minute we heard the order from the skipper was the moment I realized that we were actually going to leave the Brooklyn Navy Yard and would be on our own.

It seemed like everyday was the first time for me, and indeed it was. I was learning how to apply the knowledge I had gathered in school and every day posed a new and exciting problem to solve. At the age of seventeen, almost every event was for the first time, often leaving me bewildered if it were an emotional one. It was good to be able to reach out and ask any member of the crew their advice. I'd get the right steerage and understand how to solve it in the future. Personal problems had to be dealt with in the presence of the crew. So discipline played a big part in my life at that time.

For instance, I don't know what provoked it, but I had my first and only fist fight on board. It was amidst many of the crew. I don't really remember the fight, but I do know that it was resolved before too many blows were thrown. The crew saw to that. I remember what he looked like, vividly. I think his name was Miller. He wore glasses and had a quiet demeanor about him, sort of studious. Maybe that had something to do with it. Maybe this hayseed, didn't like the studious kind. Was this how others saw me? After all, with the exception of two months in Rye, I did come right off the farm and acted it. Matter of fact, I think I played on it.

So far in my years' career as a sailor...it wasn't yet March...I appeared to be the epitome of what people thought a sailor was. Six feet tall, still a bit gangly at 160 pounds, blond hair and blue eyes. I fit right into the Navy uniform, right down to the pea coat collar up and my little white hat rakishly over one ear...and a toothy smile. My undershot jaw gave me a pugnacious look. My top front four teeth were behind the lower teeth when I closed my mouth. Oddly enough, this genetic error would eventually lead to my being aboard this Destroyer instead of a submarine.

I actually applied for submarine service when the opportunity arose. I was really gung ho all the way. But I was refused on physical grounds; the hose to the personal escape valve was fitted to operate as soon as you bit down on it. My under bite wouldn't have accomplished that. By then I was in Norfolk and stoked on Destroyers, so I didn't mind being turned down.

So I am Norman Rockwells' vision of the United States Navy. It caused a personal problem to develop which, by its nature, did not include the crew. I noticed whenever I'd go on liberty in Manhattan, I'd be approached by a man. Once, when heading into Manhattan with my friend LeBlanc, I told him of my situation. He was nonplussed. I said, "I'll bet when we get to Times Square, if we stand on the corner, a man will approach me within ten minutes." Within five minutes after standing there, a man came up to me and said, "Excuse me, but do you have a light?" That was enough for LeBlanc. I won ten dollars.

I learned the value of hygiene aboard ship. Being a hayseed, I was brought up sharp in my algebra class at Rye High when I slipped a note to the girl next to me, asking for a date. She wrote back, "Don't you ever take a bath?" That was a good start. So, by the time I went aboard, I was already a cool dude.

We'd have discussions around the meals about the war. Everyone was so pumped up about getting the enemy. I could really care less as I was caught up in the experience of now and so much was happening that was exciting and educational that I could barely cram in each day as it arrived, with no thought at all of the future beyond the next exhilarating day.

That same shudder of the ship as the last line was thrown over, freeing the ship from earth, free to roam the planet ocean, where she really belonged. Free from the shackles binding her to planet earth. There was always that shudder of relief in release. I came to love it. The ship, for me, came to express many human sentiments in a most fascinating way.

We sailed out for the first time under the Williamsburg and the Brooklyn Bridge since half of the U.S.S. Murphy had been towed in backwards. I'm not sure if anyone on those bridges realize the significance of this voyage, but it was felt by the veterans aboard the Murphy. "You thought the Murphy had it, and we're out to show the world that nothing can beat us", must have been in the thoughts of every survivors heart.

For me, it was spectacular. It was a bright, sunny day and cold to the bone. We were at muster along the decks while we sailed out of the river and the Statue of Liberty came into sight around the corner. The biting cold only added fuel to the burning inside of me. This was the way I wanted my life to be. I was a wanderer and I was wandering. It had been only two years since I was driving a tractor on a farm and now I was sailing past the Statue of Liberty on my way to strange lands. It was all working out. I was on my way. At seventeen, I had a long way to travel.

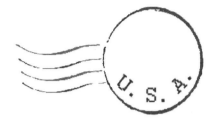

Chapter Eleven

- - - - - - - - - - - - - - - - -

At the time, we were not the only warship in the bay.
There were the unsinkable gray vessels of the Navy
scattered around the opening to the sea. There was no
Verazzano Bridge then, as we drifted past Governor's Island
and saw the Statue of Liberty off our starboard bow, we
also saw to our left, the open sea. For that was to be our
home, our planet to roam, for who knows how long.

Ferguson, a vet, was explaining ground swells to us,
which we were just beginning to feel. The ship got up to
cruising speed and we started bobbing up and down. The sea,

Ferguson explained, has its own life, apart from the waves
at the beach we were familiar with at this point. The waves
at the beach were actually earth made, in that they were
formed when approaching earth. But at sea, where there was
nothing to interfere, the sea had a life of its own,
including the making of waves. These were called ground
swells and they varied in size. We would feel them all the
way across the Atlantic.

We had been so busy securing Special Sea Detail, that
the land behind us vanished before we knew it and suddenly,
there we were at sea heading further out. Actually, we were
skirting the southern shore of Long Island on our way
eventually on to Maine. But before we could head north, we
had to get out beyond Montauk Point. Casco Bay was a
favorite spot of shakedown cruises by now, with facilities
to handle all kinds of war ships on Long Island; not the
Long Island of fame, but a little island in the bay called
locally Long Island. So everything was prepared for our
visit. We were to try out everything on board the ship,
from torpedoes to ash cans, from the five-inch guns to

twenty millimeter machine guns. We were also to check the behavior of the ship itself, by now sort of a hybrid. Would one end, the new, blend in with the old, the stern, to make a complete ship? We'd find out.

We found out in open water. Once we headed north in rising swells, the order came over the PA "Full speed ahead". We soon learned that announcing the change in speed would not ordinarily occur, because it was none of their business, those being topside. The orders to change speed came directly from the Captain to the helmsman to the engine rooms and fire rooms and the ship would shudder into a higher speed, and we'd recognize it. Full speed ahead was exhilarating at 25 miles an hour. I couldn't imagine flank speed, the all out signal. It was rumored that we could do 37 knots, about 40 miles an hour at flank speed.

First the fantail went way under the water where the screws were turning, and the bow went up in the air. Now imagine what happens to a 348 foot vessel speeding through the water. The entire fantail is under the water! While standing on the fantail by my hatch, we were several feet under the ocean level. There was a hole in the water where the stern of the ship went down for the big screws to grip. You had to run uphill if you were going anywhere forward on the ship. In other words, we acted exactly as a speed boat reacts to sudden speed. What a thrill!

The entire ship literally churned its way through the ocean, making the sounds of the screws obvious in a dull roar throughout the ship with sudden sharp reactions to the ground swells. We were going through the swells instead of going over them, an action which caused a hell of a wake and a giant dousing if you were anywhere on the bow.

Formed on the port side amid ships, the dining line, when it was a long one, sometimes extended along the gunwale. At the deck break there was a ladder down a deck to the galley. During ground swells at full speed, those on the ladder would find themselves rising uncontrollably as they literally defeated gravity and for a minute, while the ship was on the crest of a swell and would start down off it, those on the ladder would rise into the air as we came down. This made many of the men seasick before they could reach the galley.

The vets pulled a nasty trick on us greenhorns. One of them would go along the line loudly mentioning that we would be served cold pork and bacon gravy to arouse the stomachs of some of the greenhorns. It worked at least once each time. I never did get sick, although several times I witnessed the feeling.

And then there were the powdered eggs. Gross is the only word for it. They were dehydrated eggs. When mixed with water, they were ready for the frying pan. What was supposed to be scrambled eggs, turned out to be a strange mess resembling pieces of cardboard. It tasted that way too. I had come from the farm, eating fresh eggs daily, delicious fresh eggs still warm from the hen. It was a hard transition for me.

One hardy character who became famous on board was a

little, skinny guy with a great sense of humor, bless him, because every time the ship moved, every time you heard "Special Sea Detail" over the PA, Pete Karageorge would get seasick. We had a phrase on board, Up anchor, down Karageorge". But that son of a gun would not accept a transfer and suffered all the time we were at sea. He was a good sailor though, in spite of it.

There was another special thing about flank speed...you took the curves sharply. By that I mean, when the ship was cutting through swells, banging into waves, it was all done with a snap to it. You were snapped from side to side. Even in the dining line you had to keep one hand on the life line that extended up both sides of the ship, for just that. If you didn't hold onto that line, you faced going overboard. Not one person on board went over, but we saw it happen to a cruiser, three men, just like that. Hold on!

From the broken deck aft, back at the fantail, you were less than six feet to the ocean. Many times at sea, when things would get rough, I'd have to close the hatch and secure it because the ocean breached the fantail and swept across it. This was true of most of the ship from the mid superstructure on back. Incidentally, when I refer to anything superstructure, that means anything above the main deck of the ship. That includes the electricians shop.

I told Bill Snow about an article I had read in a Chicago paper when I was at Great Lakes. It was on the front page in a separate column and was titled, "Famous Last Words" and had a cute answer like, "I think it went this way". Well I had one stuck in my mind; Famous last words..."I think this wire goes here". Bill liked it so much that he had the machine shop make a little sign that said that. It hung over the electrician's shop the whole year and a half that I was on board.

There must have been a strange but effective way of timing on board ship. By that I mean, I realize I don't have any memory whatsoever of the way I slept or how I worked. It all seems to blend in. I know that the Navy operates on bells, or watches. Each watch is four hours long. The "dogwatch" was the shift between four and eight in the morning. I know I had a lot of dogwatches when we were underway and crossing the Atlantic, or in the Mediterranean, because I loved those watches. But all in all, it must have been a good system. The crew was always at its peak, the longest challenge being Normandy, when it seems I never slept nor did anyone else for nineteen days straight. Now I know we slept, but that's just my point; I can't remember when we slept, so sleep or the lack of it, never became an issue. You never heard anyone say, "I'm tired" or "I didn't get much sleep last night". When you were shaken on the shoulder from a deep sleep, that was the beginning of your watch and you got up, and as I recall, were good and awake and alert. Or maybe that's just how an eager seventeen year old works. By the way, I was the youngest on board.

What were you doing when "Station Special Sea Detail" would come over the PA? Were you just sitting around doing nothing? Was there ever such a time on board? I'm not sure. The reason being that I imagine I was so caught up in whatever I was doing, it became part of the joy of just hanging out. So the two...hanging out and working, became synonymous. I kept burning holes in my dungarees toting around all those batteries. When I needed a new pair, I knew that two weeks had passed. Life on the ocean doesn't go by days.

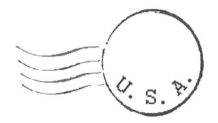

Chapter Twelve

- - - - - - - - - - - - - - - - - - -

We arrived at Long Island, Casco Bay in the dark. Scheduled for the next day were speed maneuverability trials. It was cold and there was snow on the ground. We were informed that we would get liberty around Portland when we had time.

That first day in Casco Bay dawned icy cold and gray. This was great, for it made us feel singular in the world. We cleared the dock and shuddered awake. We were doing a sprightly 10 knots until we were clear enough from land and then immediately let loose.

To say that it was exhilarating was doing a disfavor.
You wouldn't hear an astronaut describe his or her ride
into space as "exhilarating". It was so much more than
that. It was ...awesome...to stand there on the deck and
feel through your feet its trembling strength. In a
miniscule way, it's like how your first motorcycle ride
feels.

Out into the ocean was where we fired our torpedoes.
No. Fired our torpedo, for the one torpedo that we fired
that day was the only one in my entire year and a half. At
sea the torpedo mounts were together in a normal position,
all five facing forward, occupying almost the entire space
between the stacks. It was located over the machine
shop...on top of the superstructure. When we fired one, we
were at full speed. I think we kept up full speed the whole
day. The torpedo unit, including all four mounts, turned
around until the heads of the torpedoes were facing due
port, right off our beam. It came out without a bang, but
with a swoosh accompanied by something that sounded like a

bell. The torpedo was huge, belly flopping into the water and, no sooner was it under that it shot forward. You could easily see its underwater wake. I don't remember whether or not we were aiming it against anything. I just remember it shooting out over the gunwales and striking the water.

The next morning was the same weather-wise. Everything up there was gray. I decided that all of Maine was gray. Maybe this was their night. We were once again at full speed. That day, besides firing our big guns...the five-inch guns...we were to try flank speed.

Flank speed. Forever, those two words together meant power beyond necessity. The fantail during flank speed was about fifteen feet under the sea, and the body of this steed, plowing ahead, rising in defiance of the sea itself, and burying its proud head in thundering shudder, on through a swell and into the next. Flank speed.

Coming down off flank speed and back to full, we seemed for awhile to have stopped. That was an experience. The contradiction in speed was awesome. We were instructed to prepare ourselves...for a five-inch salvo or two. There was a great emphasis put on the sound we were to experience. Ear plugs of cotton were passed out by the medic. I noticed that most everyone, like me, put the cotton in their pockets. We looked forward to the complete event.

The two five-inch guns on the bow pointed directly ahead. The two aft pointed aft. If they lost power, each gun mount could rely on the storage batteries I had placed. The first gun had its powder room beneath the deck. The second gun, just forward of the pilot house, was mounted atop its powder room, which was above decks, making that gun a deck higher. Back aft, the gun closest to the fantail had its powder room below decks while the gun ahead of it had its powder room topside, making that gun a deck higher.

Now, when operated from the pilot house, all turrets moved simultaneously in the same direction. What makes this a gun instead of a rifle was the powder room. Down there, sailors handled cloth sacks filled with powder and the shells, which were heavy enough to be handled by two sailors. According to what I heard, this was a gun because it needed two things...powder and a shell, to fire. Anything of a lesser size was to be considered a rifle because the shell and the casing were together, as bullets. Ours required the same service as the big sixteen-inch guns on battleships.

The sound was truly deafening. It was a sharp crack that hurt the inner ear. So sharp that the hurt was gone instantly, but you knew the damage had been done. When they were fired in unison, you could feel the kick, and the ship could feel the kick. We braced ourselves for the salvos. Individually, it didn't kick but it seemed the noise of one equaled all four at once.

There was a target out there for us. Actually a ship, of sorts, that we could fire at. We weren't bad. We just about blew it clear out of the water. The next time we'd see shells hitting the water like that in brackets, we'd be the one bracketed by sixteen-inch German guns off

Cherbourg. Those sixteen-inchers were so big you could hear
them coming in, a great swoosh, and you could actually see
them just before they struck the water. But these five-
inchers couldn't be seen or heard. They had more of a rifle
effect.

There was a boat on Long Island which would take us
ashore for liberty. I don't recall anything about shore
leave other than meeting and sort of falling for a girl in
Portland. She was from Bangor, a sweet girl and we
corresponded for awhile after I left. I think her name was
Peggy. But all that kind of behavior was secondary to being
a sailor, and more than just a sailor, a Tin Can sailor,
although you seldom if ever heard that expression among us.
That was how other people described us.

On the third day we got to try out all the other
firearms and ash cans. That was fun because my secondary
battle station was a twenty millimeter machine gun on the
port side up alongside the torpedoes. You had to be
harnessed into a twenty millimeter. You could sort of lie

back against the harness and swivel and the gun swiveled with you. Every tenth bullet was a tracer, so you could see where you were firing. When you came away from the twenty millimeter, it took you awhile to readjust; all that noise so close by and the feeling of power surging through you as you watched tracers in the sky, going wherever you pointed, left you walking around about an inch off the deck, a little unsure of yourself in this suddenly placid world.

The forty millimeters, one on each side, up in the superstructure, were the really bi machine guns. I believe that they were the largest in size of shell. They had two barrels that pumped simultaneously, with a real thumping kind of boom. That rounded out our firepower, but we still had something for the U boats.

The ash cans were fun. They were sort of rolled over the stern and exploded at different depths somewhere not far behind us. The ones closest to the surface when they exploded were the greatest spectacle, throwing plumes of water into the sky with a deep, sonorous roar. We also had ash cans placed along the gunwales just aft of mid ship that actually shot the ash cans off the ship, them landing out about ten feet from the ship.

I was turning on to Frank Sinatra just about then. I remember "You'll Never Walk Alone" and "The House I Live In" very well, although there was no romance involved. I always had a love of music and had learn the harmonica when I'd walk up into the pasture after the cows. And of course, I'd experienced the likes of Duke Ellington and had even danced to the band.

When I was attending Rye High School, our music teacher, Doc Mize was a friend of Dukes and offered our school auditorium for his Carnegie Hall dress rehearsal. They sold tickets and packed the house. Duke was having so much fun, he suggested that the music continue in the gymnasium later that night and we all danced the night away. That was the night that he introduced "Mood Indigo" and "Satin Doll" including "Black, Brown and Beige". I was awed. As if it were last night I can still hear the sweet, rolling song of John Hodges' alto, the incredibly moving arrangements of the various sections. I remember hearing Juan Tizol and Tricky Sam Nanton (the first time I ever heard such muting); falling in love with the jazz violin, played by Ray Nance, who also played clarinet; hearing a great trumpet player named Rex Stewart.

The female vocalist was Betty Roche and of course, the drummer was Sonny Greer. I had volunteered as a make-shift waiter, serving cokes and such around the gymnasium, and got to stand right next to the band most of the night. I even got to pick up one of Greer's sticks and handed it back to him. He hung out with me and my buddy Nemo during their break. He asked us where he could get a drink. So we took him upstairs to our lockers and delivered him a half-pint of Apple Jack.

Meanwhile, the shakedown cruise was a huge success. The skipper was thrilled with the outcome and we sailed back to New York and past the Statue of Liberty a proud ship that was together in every way imaginable. We were to stay there only one month. In that month, I had my eighteenth

birthday, practically unnoticed in the big Brooklyn Navy

Yard. There was a lot of talk going on; not about the ship,

but about the war. We now knew that we were ready for it

and our interest changed. Now we were facing the next step,

and that war over there, across the ocean, was our next

step. I felt it ironic that I had been preparing all this

time and now that I was eighteen, it was time to go.

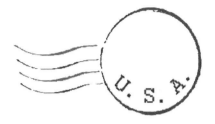

Chapter Thirteen

- - - - - - - - - - - - - - - - - - - -

A lot had happened in that first year. A lot more was about to happen as we set sail for Ireland. I can't remember much of the trip over. It probably took about ten days to cross the Atlantic, as we traveled in a convoy. We, the sailors, never kept those kinds of records. We just sailed along, from one place to another. Not necessarily one port to another. Much of our time was spent, not in port, but in the waters outside of places like Normandy, or southern France.

I recall that I came topside from sleep to find myself

in the harbor of Belfast, North Ireland. It was my first look at foreign soil. It was the fourth of April, 1944. Looking around I realized we were part of a huge flotilla of all kinds of ships in the harbor. We were anchored out about a half mile from the shore, and already the dinghies and other sized boats were plying the waters among the big ships. I saw the heavy cruiser Augusta, looking sleek and old fashioned with her heavily raked bow. I think the British cruiser Ajax was there, along with an inordinate number of smaller, maritime ships.

We were given liberty and went ashore in the whaleboats. I met a girl there and I loved hearing her say "Robert Perham. U.S.S. Murphy DD603". That doesn't mean much to the reader, but as I wrote it I remembered exactly how she had said it, with the most beautiful lilting Irish accent I've ever heard since. I learned that, according to legend, Irish girls can get it on when standing up, like in a doorway, because they believe you have to lie down to commit a sin. Well, I didn't try any of that. I was too busy being a Tin Can sailor.

The three days we spent in Ireland were fraught with preparations. We stocked up our refrigerator and got caught up with shells for the guns. I checked every battery on board and the head set system was checked out and working. At that time, we had head sets that connected us to every important person on the ship. The head sets were voice activated, a recent invention and a great energy saver.

We went out a couple of days and sailed up and down the Irish Sea, once getting close to the Scottish shoreline and seeing some of the Firths as well as the heavily treed and bright green countryside going right down to waters edge. Stunningly beautiful. Eventually, we sailed south down the Irish Sea and past the Isle of Man, around the corner of England and to Plymouth.

The port of Plymouth was deep with a narrow entrance. Its entrance was impressive for all the ships there. Immediately outside the harbor seemed almost chaotic. There were boats of every description everywhere. As we got deeper into the port, we realized those ships were out there because there was no longer any room further in. In short, the port was full of ships.

The city was pretty crowded, too. In the harbor there were sunken ships here and there. In the city there were plenty of street corners, plenty of street blocks actually, that had been bombed out and the rubble piled up. There were signs everywhere about rats. Rats were the big cause for alarm. I remember because I saw a rat amidst a pile of rubble and raced after it, clubbing it to death in front of a bunch of appreciative residents. I was a hero that day in Plymouth.

I looked at a map and figured out how far I could go in a day on the train heading north into the country. The place was Saint Germain. So I got a ticket and spent the day in the English countryside in Saint Germain and Tavistock. The trains were marvelous. Narrow gauge and fancy, a great way to travel. I had fish and chips for the first time and was surprised to find that English people, most of them around Plymouth anyway, had a way with the word "fuck". It seemed like a common curse word to them. It came out about every four sentences, casually. I was surprised. I guess by then I had this idea of stodginess associated with the British.`

We sailed out of Plymouth several times while we were there. We were now aware that something was about to happen and we were to be part of it. For the first time, we felt that all this, from Casco Bay on, was leading up to something mighty big. But even then, we weren't sure. But this crowding of harbors wasn't normal. There were too many ships, it seemed, everywhere we went. The channel was crowded each time that we went out there.

We went out a number of times. Up the Irish Sea again, not so far this time, holding maneuvers up and down the coast, occasionally spotting the Isle of Man. Thus a month passed and the excitement kept building without a comment from anyone. It was just that everywhere we went now, there seemed to be other ships around. Finally, on the fourth of June, we pulled out of Plymouth harbor for the last time, and we knew it. Somehow the message had been delivered: this is it. This is what all these ships have been waiting for. As we pulled out of the Plymouth harbor, we felt it closing behind us. Every ship that had been crowded into Plymouth harbor was moving out with us. I doubt that there was a ship left by the time we sailed out into the crowded English Channel.

At first, we encountered an unfriendly wind that started almost as soon as we left the harbor. We plowed on, with fair weather as far as the sky was concerned but the wind brought heavy swells and it soon became a wet voyage. Within the hour, more than the wind had whipped up. The sea was now in a fury. We had with us the British cruisers Ajax and Achilles, and once, when I ventured outside from the engine room, I saw the Ajax practically climb up the side of a wave so steep that I could clearly see the lines of the wooden deck. It was time to hold on tight. This had become a major storm. We were rolling through the heaviest weather we'd been in so far. Suddenly the sea took center stage and whatever we'd been heading for was on hold. We turned back only to learn that Plymouth harbor had indeed been closed and we rode out most of the storm in the English Channel.

We eventually made our way back to Portland Bill and Weymouth which were closer to London, about half way from Plymouth, where we struggled to find space to tie up and hardly spent time there at all before Ike Eisenhower came over every PA in the Navy. He told us that this was it. This would be the biggest invasion in history and we were to be part of it. "Godspeed" and we were once more on our way.

Crossing the Channel in perfect weather, it looked like you could jump from ship to ship all the way to the horizon, on both sides. There were little blimps on the bow of most of the maritime ships. They were tethered at about fifty feet above the ships. We were told that they were to ward off strafing planes. It seems that all the way over, we heard the drone of airplanes as huge numbers of them passed us by on their way to the mainland, all kinds. Over a hundred B-17's passed over. They were followed by several hundred fighter planes; all with their undersides painted a striped black and white. There were P-38's, Mustangs and P-40's, as well as some P-47 Thunderbolts. There were every kind of English and American fighter planes. It seemed like a planet of planes to us. But then, we were blanketing the surface of the Channel so completely, that we seemed to move with the earth.

We arrived off the coast of Normandy around ten o'clock. I had become used to the long days in June this far north. I once read the paper while standing on deck at ten at night. Already we hear the distant thunder of guns coming from far inland. That would probably be the gliders, the first to hit enemy lines, actually behind the lines. We found out later that many of the gliders flipped over on landing. I later found out the "Rabbit" Ralph Blohm, one of the three that I had enlisted with, was among those glider soldiers who didn't survive the attack.

We were ordered in at about one in the morning. By now

the thunder of war had increased and the troops were starting to hit the beach. We were now about five hundred yards off shore. This area was known as Omaha Beach. That night we didn't fire our five-inchers. We stood off and watched the LCVP's, gliding by in the darkness. It was a gruesome sight for all of us, feeling safe in the bowels of our ship. We watched wave after wave of LVCP's, barely out of the water, slide by loaded to the gunwales with soldiers. These soldiers were so packed in that they weren't allowed to leave their boats during the storm, which postponed this whole thing by twenty four hours. Those soldiers had stood in those boats, riding the storm, probably barfing on the man in front, and then were taken into shore and dumped off in the darkness and cold water. We watched them chug by and realized the profundity of war as they hit the beach. By now, the sky was glowing orange with thousands of tracer bullets, and we were overwhelmed with a barrage of sound. We were moved to tears as we watched these guys bravely face incredible hardships, and felt guilty to be safely on board ship. These soldiers, these young men, were already exhausted before they hit their destination.

Steven Spielberg's "Saving Private Ryan" was, in my
estimation, the only film made since "All Quiet On The
Western Front" that depicted war the way that I remember
it. Unrelenting. The sound never stopped. It was the sound
of thousands of tracer bullets filling the sky. Every
night, for the nineteen nights that we were there, the sky
turned orange with tracer bullets. You could just imagine
the sounds. Everyday it seemed, we were strafed at least
once, and that gave me the chance to fire my twenty
millimeter. At night they'd fly over and drop mines in the
area. The Nelson, a ship in our squadron , eventually
backed into one of those mines. We were constantly on alert
for the mines and the German E boats that delivered them.
The E boats were slightly larger than our PT boats and just
as fast. They came slithering in the night. We could hear
them.

The first day of the invasion the sun came up over a
dark and littered sea. This convinced me with a chill that

we could indeed get into trouble. Starting then and for several days, we wandered about, pulling bodies from the water. That first day we had seven stacked up on the bow until a PT boat, stopping at each ship, took them aboard for ultimate burial. Everything floated by. The surface was littered. Off in the distance was the Augusta, the flag ship of this operation, upon which General Omar Bradley directed his troops. It was unharmed. But next to us, the Nelson and the Glennon were out of commission; both of them down at the stern.

We received orders to come close to shore and to zero in on a church steeple in a small town named Mers Ste Igles. From a few hundred yards off shore, we fired several salvos from our five-inch guns, clearly taking the top of the church steeple off. That was when I actually witnessed my first casualty of the war. I was watching the church through a set of binoculars that I had borrowed from one of the quartermasters up by the pilot house. I focused on the church. It was before we fired anything. An American GI came into view and stood there, obviously peeing. I had half a smile on my face when the soldier, in the midst of peeing, suddenly fell forward and lay there, motionless. Several minutes later we fired at the church. The soldiers on the ground didn't move.

For some reason I remember vividly the gunnery officer getting on the PA before the invasion and saying that we should dress warmly and comfortably because it may be days before we'll get a chance to change; "We'll be at our battle stations at all times, during and after the invasion." As a result, I wore the same long johns for eighteen days straight...a record I've never broken since.

I'm trying to recreate those days at Normandy, but they seem pretty much to meld all together. One obvious reason for that was being at our battle stations. That meant, for all intents and purposes, that I would spend four hours on watch in the steering engine room and would go immediately to my battle station thereafter.

The Germans ME-109 was our nemesis. In the first place,

it looked a lot like a Spitfire or P-40. Believe me, it was a smart thing to paint the undersides of all allied planes with black and white broad stripes. We were constantly on the look out for strafers; single planes that suddenly appeared out of nowhere and sent shrapnel and panic topside. I made a habit of strapping myself into the machine gun and when I relaxed, backwards, the strap held me and the gun pointed skyward. I was thus hanging from my gun, when out of nowhere came the ME-109. I fired like mad, watching my tracers, leading him as he veered upward and, smoking, as he vanished into some clouds. There were dozens of machine guns, there always were, and it was impossible to tell who hit him, but from then on, when discussing my machine gun I'd always say, "One of them was smoking when I fired", as if saying it proved me a good shot.

In the first three days we lost four of our eight squadron members. The Nelson backed into a mine, the Jeffers was shot out of commission as was the Plunkett, while the Glennon had suffered major hits.

I kept a diary of the entire invasion. It was 265 pages of hand printed words in four little black books. It would be wonderful if they were found. They were last seen in our house on Amestoy Street in Encino, California, where we lived the last years that I was married. I remember passages from it, but not the days. I remember writing..."Tonight was a particularly busy one...I saw six planes go down". You might wonder how I managed to keep score at night, but I had a system. Like I said, the sky often turned completely orange with tracer bullets. When a spot in the sky flared up and then started down, you figured it to be a plane. Speaking of my diary and passages remembered, I recall looking first to me right and then to my left and writing, "It looks like a huge carnival as we occupy the entire Channel with ships and balloons. Hitler will have a different word for it...he'll call it carnage." I was barely eighteen then.

On the fifth or sixth day, we received mail! Can you believe it? We were astonished and thrilled as we realized that the PT boat pulling up alongside of us had a different mission this time. The bodies had all been picked up. A

chief petty officer climbed up the side of our ship

carrying a huge bag of mail. I received a half of dozen

letters. One was a sweet letter from Peggy, whom I'd never

see again, and one was from my sister Pat with news of her

night out at the Paramount with Frank Sinatra. In the

middle of all this madness, we got mail!

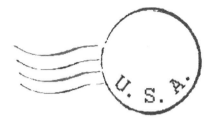

Chapter Fourteen

_ _ _ _ _ _ _ _ _ _ _ _ _ _ _ _ _

What I remember most about Normandy was the mess. That is what Speilberg got so well. I felt as I sat through "Saving Private Ryan" that it would never end; I wasn't even sure if Tom Hanks' character was alive or dead at the end of the film. It didn't matter. In war, nothing matters and the whole thing is a mess. A human mess. Bodies floating everywhere and the entire surface of the water disturbed by flotsam...and it was our job to sort through it all. During the first few days, enduring such a gruesome task, we pulled up a case of whiskey from the dirty water and it was immediately taken down to sick bay. The doctor prescribed two or three drinks per person...I don't know

how much the officers got, but the crew of the U.S.S.

Murphy was definitely drunk for one day during the invasion

and it was a welcomed deviation for all of us.

There was something happening all the time, twenty four

hours a day. We spent a lot of time at battle stations and

sleep was not figured in. You got it when you found time to

get it. I was mostly awake. I can't remember going to my

bunk and getting sleep, although I must have done it

sometime. Sleeping would have been difficult as there was

never a lull in the noise of war.

There was never a lull in our movement either. In fact,

I don't remember the anchor being dropped even once. We

were moving all the time. On the second or third day, we

went over to Gold Beach, which consisted of mostly Canadian

troops. It was there, or Juneau Beach, where most of the

French fleet was operating. Those French ships were

magnificent. Only the Augusta in the American fleet had the

lines of almost every French ship I saw during WWII. They

had severely raked bows, making them look as if they could definitely cut through the ocean. In fact, probably as much a matter of show biz, at one point a French Destroyer circled us at over thirty knots! We were really impressed. The French Destroyers were larger than ours and looked stronger. We used to enjoy calling the French "frogs".

Don't ask me why. We didn't call the English "limeys", but we made sure that every Frenchman was a "frog". Oddly enough, I can't remember what we called the Germans.

By the time we returned back to Omaha Beach, the fighting had become sparse. The allied troops had pushed inland. So on the eighteenth day...we left. Imagine how we must have felt as we steamed out to sea and away from the war torn France. Little did we realize at the time within two months, we'd be hitting the shores of France once more. We crossed an empty Channel, smooth in the late June sunlight, arriving while still light, about nine or ten that evening, and tied up to, off all things, an aircraft carrier. Oh, this was too much!

These long johns came off and I entered a long line at the showers but it was more than worth it. It was like cleaning off after a hard day's work on the farm. We felt gratified and were thrilled when invited on board the carrier. I don't remember its name. I'm not sure I got it even then, because we were as if in heaven...a Naval heaven...but heaven just the same. Not only did they serve gee dunk, (nomenclature for ice cream), but they had a bar from which to serve it. It was like coming in from a mess of work, cleaning up and going to heaven.

Heaven was a little city of over three thousand people, mostly smiling and frightfully dressed, and like angels they all had smiles. I think all I did for some time was walk, walk, walk through the passageways. I had no idea of feeling trapped while onboard my ship, but now this ability to walk, walk, walk, was a definite thrill. I almost got lost trying to get back on board my ship. There were so many decks in heaven!

Back to the business of war, we spent the next day reloading the ship with everything from food to ammunition. During the eighteen days, several of us managed to find a way into the walk-in refrigerator and I, for one, would eat only the big heads of lettuce, cold and with sugar. I would eat a whole head at a time, with nothing but sugar on it.

We had to reload all four of the five-inch guns. We needed ammunition for both the twenty millimeters and the forty millimeters. I don't remember any threats of U boats While we were at Normandy, so the ash cans were still intact, along with the five torpedoes. Toward the end of the day, it became apparent to most of us that we were working against the clock and that somehow we were going to get in trouble again and very soon, perhaps even the next day.

I recall waking up to Special Sea Detail early the next morning. As we sailed out of Portland Bill, we were joined by some familiar and imposing company; the battleship Nevada and heavy cruiser Quincy were there, along with several British cruisers the Ajax and the Achilles. In any case, this was an imposing fleet.

Before leaving, the carriers huge green Shamrocks were riveted to both sides of the after stacks, which made us the only ship with a logo.

Crossing the English Channel was different than the last time. We had nothing but naval power this time...no liberty ships. In fact, we were the smallest vessel in this fleet; Destroyers and Battleships and several Cruisers. There was armour consisting of everything up to sixteen-Inch guns on the Nevada, and believe me, that day we saw all those guns in action...scary action. I still couldn't believe that our ship was untouched and that our crew was still intact.

It was the twenty fifth of June. We were heading for Cherbourg, several miles down the coast from Normandy. We found out from our Chief Gunnery Officer what this was all about. Cherbourg is located at the point of land jutting out into the English Channel. It seems our troops, on invading Normandy, had gone south and around the Peninsula to Cherbourg, a big French port city. But when starting toward Cherbourg, our soldiers were met by huge fire from the guns of Cherbourg. These were guns as large as sixteen-inchers, the size of Nevada's guns. It was even rumored that the guns were eighteen inches in diameter, making them the largest that we had ever heard of. The Germans turned the guns from the ocean to the east, where they were firing at, and stopping the invasion into France. So we were ordered to turn those big guns back around, firing out to sea. We were to be the targets.

It was exciting for its cleanliness, as compared to Normandy. There was no mess here. The Channel, as we approached land, was clear and serene on a beautiful June day. Suddenly, it seemed that all the naval ships began speeding up and down the Channel, inviting attack. It was, for lack of a better word, fun. We raced back and forth along the shoreline at a distance.

Every ship was doing the same thing, running at flank speed back and forth along the coast, churning up the sea. The reactions were to be expected. Before we knew it, we were bracketed by huge shells. It was terrifying. We fired our five-inch guns, uselessly. They probably reached shore. The Nevada's guns were magnificent. This great size of the guns presented an incredible sight at sea.

We could actually hear and see the brackets as they flew overhead and splashed into the water. I was up at the searchlight and saw what the beginning of a bracket was. Just the thought of one of those shells hitting us was enough, but to hear they whistle like a freight train overhead and splash into the sea with such force was stunning and it took a few days to come down from the experience.

A big splash on our starboard side and...hang on...a big splash on our port side, actually less than twenty yards away, which left me soaking wet, but jubilant because they missed us completely. If you could hear the sound and see the ships speeding by, this carnival scene was an awesome sight. We churned through endless wakes, riding the offspring of the bigger ships.

We succeeded in turning the big guns around and had them aimed at us instead of the land troops, allowing them to push further into the city. For over three hours we were not sitting, but running ducks, back and forth, invoking brackets of fire. This was the most exciting time of my life. I was scared to death and I believed that we were all very close to dying. This was purely a Naval engagement. Three hours and forty five minutes of this concentrated activity, made the eighteen days at Normandy seem docile in comparison. According to our gunnery officer, the Nevada sent one shell directly through the slot of a gun turret, blowing up one gun and taking up enough time for the troops to move even further in. After three hours and forty five minutes, we sailed out and away from Cherbourg, once again untouched.

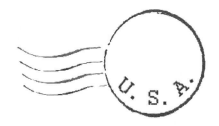

Chapter Fifteen

- - - - - - - - - - - - - - - - -

We spent the next several days back in Portland Bill. Heaven wasn't there anymore. Just the idea of truly relaxing around the ship finally sank in, and we spent the next week doing just that. After sewing up some loose ends, we found ourselves shoving off once again.

This time the route was south, and as of lately, somewhat fraught. Since we would sail through the Bay of Biscayne on our way to the Mediterranean Sea, we were instructed to keep an eye out for the Graf Spee; the most feared German heavy cruiser, thought to be hiding somewhere in the bay. That put an edge on an otherwise serene voyage.

We were breathing easier when we entered the Mediterranean Sea, as we had gotten word that the Graf Spee was caught in a harbor in France or Germany.

By the time we entered the Mediterranean, the night sky had filled with brilliant stars. Every other light in the world was subdued from wartime blackouts and brownouts. (As a matter of fact, no light was ever visible topside on our ship. It was equipped with switches at each hatchway to automatically turn off the second a door was opened. Under no circumstances were you allowed to have a visible light topside. If you smoked, you lit your cigarette with a lighter that was a rope with an embering end. And even those had to be cupped in your fist.)

My diary of the first night in the Mediterranean included the following: "It was an unusually starry night tonight. I saw two shooting stars in five minutes." It truly was something awesome...until we discovered what phosphorous meant. Actually, phosphorous was so thick when we entered the Mediterranean, that we had fun back aft where we were about six feet from the ocean. Huge chunks of phosphorous washed up onto the deck. As it slid around we would grab handfuls and throw it at one another.

Well, those clever Germans. In the darkened sea, we churned up the phosphorous in our wake, leaving a glowing arrow trail behind us. Now the Germans, being smart, sent Stuka dive bombers out into the night over the Mediterranean. They'd fly until they saw a phosphorous arrow. They knew that at the end of that arrow was a ship, an enemy ship. So they would fly over, quite high and out of earshot, and suddenly, where the arrow of phosphorous ended, they'd dive.

We were heading for Oran, North Africa. I had taken to sleeping outdoors; up by the thirty-six inch searchlight where there was some space to lie down. Around the ship, at strategic spots, was a dispenser of sorts. It had the means of survival if there were ever a gas attack. Included with the gas masks were the sheets of waterproof, light canvas. They were large enough to cover several bodies to protect from falling gas.

There was no plastic in those days. So this was special...a blanket that was light but strong enough to protect us. I pulled one of those "blankets" out of its place and used it as a cover when sleeping topside. It was perfect...it kept the constant spray off me, so I could actually sleep up there without getting wet and cold. It was a magnificent position; it provided me with comfort while topside and kept me near my searchlight, which was my area during battle stations. We hardly expected any of that as we sped through the Mediterranean on our way down to Africa.

I wasn't asleep at the time. It was difficult to sleep with so many stars. The night sky was such a thick blanket, that it cast light across the surface of the sea, almost enough light to see us from a distance. But it was the wake that a German dive bomber saw. Suddenly it dived to release its bomb. Until that dive, the earth had been peaceful, actually beautiful in its simplicity. The only sound was the throbbing of our mighty engines and the slap of water against the sides of the ship, now plowing along at about 15 knots. I was nearly asleep when suddenly, on this beautiful, quiet night, came the distant sound of the call to battle stations.

It was a clanging sound that was clearly heard throughout the ship. It kept clanging away until we were all charged with its sound. By now, that sound brought us to an immediate fighting spirit. My being topside that night, I could just imagine that everyone was rolling out of their bunks in a controlled panic, already cursing the enemy before their feet hit the deck. I rolled out from my canopy totally discombobulated, this time not cursing the enemy but swearing under my breath that this wasn't supposed to be happening. Something must have gotten into the sound mechanism and set off that terrifying clanging in the middle of the night, under thousands of stars, in the middle of the Mediterranean Sea no less.

Before I hit the deck, I heard it. It was a whining

sound, different than battle stations and suddenly very frightening. Then there was the explosion, not far off our port beam, shattering the darkness with a blinding flash that accompanied the explosion. The ship shuddered. All hands were running to their stations instinctively, still wondering what in the hell had happened. What had happened was that the radar had spotted the Stukas, there were more than one, and the skipper realized we were a sitting duck on the surface. The skipper had ordered all engines stopped, and a hard right rudder. Once the engines had stopped, the hard right rudder had forced us into a semi-circular slide through the water. We ended up about fifty yards from the end of the phosphorous ribbon. The Stuka had dropped his bomb and it landed right where we had been, at the end of the telltale ribbon.

That was it. The Stukas left as if they had assumed that they had made a direct hit. I was notified later, that each Stuka had but one bomb, a big one, to drop. Once done, hit or miss, they started home. Of course, they left us in a shamble of nerves. None of us went back to bed at all that night, and it was a pretty tired crew that sailed the U.S.S. Murphy into the North African port of Oran. As we drifted into port, under a cloudless, hot, dry sun, we struck upon a huge sunken warship just off the port. It was a reminder to us that we were, indeed, in a war that had been fought for a couple years already. It truly was a "World War". From then on, every port we hit had evidence of prior destruction.

This must have been an intense memory for the veterans onboard. The Murphy's first wartime battle had been on these beaches. Both the ship and the crew were severely damaged. The crew managed to patch up the leak and continue fighting off an air attack on Fedhala before heading home to Boston for repairs. This was November 1942, less than a year and a half before Normandy.

Oran was peaceful, at least enough for liberty in town. Nomenclature defines an overnight or two pass a "liberty", whereby anything longer than that is called "leave". For a kid of eighteen, I'd already seen England, been to France after a fashion, and now I was mingling with North Africans in Mers El Kebir, a suburb of Oran. The coastline and the cities were dry, dusty, and hot. One of the things that stand out in my mind; there was a line formed on the outskirts of town. It was a huge long line of sailors, with a few soldiers mixed in. The line was to a favorite brothel in town.

Before leaving the ship, the Executive Officer got on the PA system and warned us of behavior detrimental to the uniform we were wearing. Why, then, I questioned, were there sailor MP's controlling the line? It was definitely "off bounds" for us, but it was controlled by MP's. I found that arguable and realized the hypocrisy of rules.

Oh yes, the wagons! There were very pretty horse drawn wagons with their windows covered in black. They also made up a line to the brothel. I don't think I ever got in that line of sailors, because I'm sure I would have remembered that. But thank goodness because I didn't have to fear the diseases so many warned about.

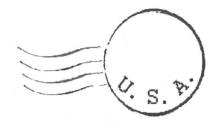

Chapter Sixteen

- - - - - - - - - - - - - - - - - -

After a few days we left Oran and sailed out to sea once again. Once we were off, we were told that we were going to another invasion, this time to southern France. We were heading to the area of France where Toulon and Marseilles were.

Sailing across the Mediterranean in the daylight was glorious. The Mediterranean was an experience in itself. In 1944 it was pristine. The colors of the water were breathtaking. We passed through the Straights of Gibralter at night. We knew that we had left the Atlantic Ocean and that we had entered something. It was special alright. So beautiful, there were times when I found myself gasping at the beauty. Dolphins swam with the ship, obviously happy to have this aquatic heaven to play in.

By the time we arrived off the coast of southern France, we were in no mood to fight, but the sight of what we were assigned to do in this invasion was spectacular. We approached nine of the strangest ships ever built during WWII. We saw nine aircraft carriers. Wait! They weren't carriers. They seemed to be Liberty ships. Liberty ships were well known by now, taking up the bulk of any convoy. They weren't Navy. They were merchant ships rebuilt with a flat area across the superstructure for planes to land and take off. We were to defend them and their leader; the aircraft carrier that we had boarded, the one we called "heaven".

This was a completely different assignment than the one we had at Normandy. Actually, it turned out to be fun because, like the "carriers", we had to remain quite a distance off shore. We were to protect the ships and at the same time, rescue downed planes in the water. The "fun" we had was watching the planes hit the water, something they were not designed to do. It turned out that some of the pilots of returning planes must have looked down on the tiny surface they were to land on and, remembering how it was when they took off, barely making it, and deciding that it was much easier to ditch the plane in the ocean and be picked up by us. As a result, we spent most of the invasion of southern France moving fast around the sea, waiting for planes to hit the water and then dragging the pilot out before he sank with the ship.

We saw every kind of plane hit the water. As I remember, the ones that really made a splash were the P-47 Thunderbolts. The had a huge engine mounting and they really hit the water hard. Mustangs were another problem, with their air scoops underneath their belly, but we managed to save every pilot except one. We weren't there when some of them splashed down, but were there shortly afterward. Once, when approaching a downed plane, we discovered that, somehow, the pilot's chute had opened. We got there in time to see, in the crystal clear water, the

pilot's body, dangling at the ends of his parachute,

inflated and billowing out under the surface of the water.

We arrived too late for that one.

But we arrived in time for everyone else. We were kept

running at flank speed, in short bursts, zigzagging across

the sea, saving pilots from watery graves. As a result, we

entered quite a few ports along the south coast of France.

Once we sailed into Marseilles and then we visited Toulon,

a port I'll never forget.

When the French surrendered to the Germans, the bulk of

the French fleet was in Toulon. Rather than give themselves

over to the Germans, the French scuttled almost their

entire fleet right there in Toulon harbor. I wonder if

they're still there as we saw them, sticking out of the

water, some of them sunk to the pilot house, an entire row

where only the masts were visible, row upon row of masts

sticking out of the water. It was eerie, and it showed the

cost of war. I thought of those pretty French ships at

Normandy and wished they had all survived. It was a sad day in Toulon.

Once we had to chase a plane down at San Tropez. We actually came so close to shore that we pulled into San Tropez and docked amid a fleet of PT boats. For once, we were the big ship in port, and the PT sailors were all over us, letting us have souvenirs that they had picked up along the way. They gave us ash trays and Nazi insignia memorabilia. It was a party atmosphere, as some of the PT sailors even had drinks. Since that time I have marveled over the success of San Tropez, especially since Brigit Bardot moved there and made it famous.

Something happened in 1968, while I was an actor, Jeremy Slate, playing a role in a wartime movie, "The Devil's Brigade", with William Holden. It was a true story about a special brigade which achieved tremendous success at Italy's Salerno and Anzio. They also suffered quite a loss. They were affectionately known as "The Devil's Brigade", something the German's had named them. I was talking to the author of the book from which the film was based, and he mentioned going into France. "But", he hastened to explain, "it was something special for us. We had to be moved in by parachute and they had built these aircraft carriers from which we were to take off." I was dumbstruck.

When I told him what we did there, he was amazed that we got together again. Here, almost thirty years later, on a set of the movie depicting their talents. Small world. I don't know what happened to those nine ships. I never heard about them after that. Maybe the Navy didn't want to be reminded.

I don't know where those ships went, but I remember where we went. We went sailing across an incredibly beautiful sea, toward Italy. The route took us through the most beautiful day I ever spent aboard ship; the Straits of Sardinia. We sailed, still with "heaven" and some of the other carriers, first to Ajaccio, Corsica, where it was rumored that there was a German boat of one size or another in the port of Ajaccio, and it ruled the roost there. The U.S.S. Murphy was sent in to challenge it and exchange gunfire along the way.

But we didn't budge the Germans, and we sailed on, catching up with the carriers in the Straits between Corsica and Sardinia. Looking back, this truly was a magnificent day. The sea was glassy, the weather incredibly perfect, and the carriers, sliding through the Straits, would turn one way and then the other. They skid through the water, and made the surface behind them glassy and smooth. The surface reflected the sun and made one look with wonder at both sides of the Straits, making Corsica and Sardinia two of the most beautiful places this side of heaven. As a matter of fact, where I live now, nestled amongst the Redwoods of California in Big Sur. I'm occasionally reminded of that day in 1944.

On the other side of Corsica and Sardinia, the U.S.S. Murphy sailed on, alone, and entered the port of Naples, Italy, about four days after the troops had taken it back from the Germans. I was able to go ashore in Naples. I remember walking through the narrow streets with the laundry hanging out. There weren't many people visible and those who were looked as if they'd seen war. The city was in shambles but maintained, somehow, the spirit of a great community that would once rise again. I walked through a large park along the waterfront and saw several people sleeping in the street. The next day I was told that all those sleeping bodies were dead bodies. They lay all around the city and were collected each morning.

It was eerie. This Italy was not like the Italy I had read about. This Italy had few Italians visible. It had been four days since they were freed from the Nazis, and they still stayed inside...or died outside in the streets to be carried away like garbage the next morning. It wasn't what I had expected, but I definitely knew that I was in Italy, and I was absorbing the city differently than Plymouth, England or Belfast, North Ireland.

We saw, but didn't visit, the Isle of Capri. I had

known about that romantic place from the song..."Twas on the Isle of Capri that I met her...", but it seemed perverse to think about visiting Capri at this time. We stayed, anchored out, for two days, then got underway, heading south to Salerno and Anzio; two little port cities that had become internationally known in the past few weeks due to the invasion of Italy by American troops. This is where they entered Italy, and then four days later, they moved up and took Naples.

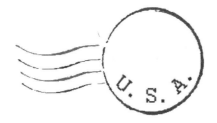

Chapter Seventeen

- - - - - - - - - - - - - - - - - -

We arrived in the port of Salerno, where it was definitely crowded. There were ships everywhere, or should I say boats. According to nomenclature, a boat was a vessel capable of being carried, while it was a ship that did the carrying. This port seemed filled with LCVP's, LST's and a few mine sweepers. I liked the mine sweepers. There were two kinds; the regular resembled a tug, flat bowed and of sturdy design. I liked those. Then there was the ocean going mine sweep, the kind that I saw in Salerno, just much larger.

On board one of those mine sweeps, I knew, was my favorite cousin, Russell. I knew about him because just weeks before he had received a medal for his performance in saving some Marines during the invasion. I can't remember where I had heard it, but going into Salerno, I knew I might just find him...and I did.

The port was so busy and we were busy also, rearming ourselves and refueling. The best I could do was to go up to a wing on the bridge facing Russell's boat, and with permission from the quartermaster, used the light to signal him...in Morse code. By flipping a cover on the light you could signal Morse...one short and one long. Sure enough, Russell was on board the vessel. I got Russell! I don't remember a word that we said. It must have been something, with him just having won a medal, and me having just survived Normandy, but I can't remember a word of it. I can't remember the name of his mine sweeper either.

It's funny; I remember faces and names of certain individuals like it was yesterday. Joe Buck, Charlie

Pottorf, Joe Rachon, Pete Karageorge, Henry George, and Ferguson and Jacobson from the old vets, of course Bill Snow, the head electrician who took a liking to me. I don't know why their names stand out in my memory, but they do, and their faces too, and their voices.

Charlie Robinson had a hard time with his voice. He was striking for quartermaster and was obliged to use the PA system once in a while. He'd come on, "Now here this ...station special detail..." and the titters would start around the ship, as Charlie sounded very effeminate. I remembered my experience in New York. I felt close to Charlie for his needless suffering. I was more with him than the rest of the crew, which made me think of myself and wonder. We sailed south through the Straits of Messina, which was a very exciting voyage for me. Being a huge fan of fireworks since childhood, I was thrilled to see the biggest of them all. Off to our right, over on Sicily, Mount Etna was doing her thing in a big way. The sky glowed orange just like it had at Omaha beach. This glow evoked a different feeling, one of awe instead of fear.

The old vets must have had a twinge as they passed by Sicily. Just a year ago, in August of 1943, the Murphy was hit in the stern and dive bombed while on duty.

It seems we were determined to stop and visit every island in the Mediterranean, and now it was time for the smallest one. Malta is located south of Sicily. We would be passing by on our way back to Oran. We knew we were heading back, but we didn't realize that we'd be treated to such a world tour. In retrospect, I thank Royal Wolverton, our skipper. He was the one educating us. Maneuvered us into all these ports. "Let's give these youngsters a trip they'll never forget", I can just hear him saying. I was blessed, as was everyone on the Murphy. Hell, the Murphy itself was blessed.

So we stopped at Malta. Malta consists of two tiny islands, yet it is considered a nation. We visited both islands while we were there. I remember that it was the most bombed of every place in the Mediterranean. Why would anyone want to bomb this island so much. One rumor had it that the tiny islands had been bombed over four hundred times. It must have had to do with jettisoning. Bombers returning to the mainland from having bombed, say, Oran, jettisoned whatever they had left over Malta, on their way home. That was the only solution I could come up with. But war is stupid anyway, so this is just one more example of its stupidity.

We moored at Valletta, the first island and went ashore. I recall eating at an outdoor restaurant on a sunny, hot dry day. I was attracted to two men that sat at the next table. They were eating the nuts that were on every table as an appetizer, When the men cracked the nuts, it sounded as if something was breaking. It was breaking all right. You knew from the sound and the self congratulatory smiles on their faces this was a challenge; to break the shell of these nuts with their teeth.

The sound was obvious. I wouldn't dare try it. Okay, I did, with no results. That is, I knew enough to stop before exerting the strength to break one of my teeth...and I let it go at that. The two men seemed delighted with me for trying. That's what I remember about Malta. The fact that it was bombed four hundred times so far and had nuts that were a challenge to crack. From there we visited the other island and its capitol.

We left Malta and headed southwest, diagonally across the Mediterranean, toward Oran. That night we were moving at a leisurely full speed, ten or more knots, on a relatively easy sea, with smooth long lasting ground swells. I was on my watch in the after steering room. I was in immediate contact with the bridge through new, voice activated head phones. I don't recall who was on the bridge at the time, but through persuasive conversation I was allowed to take over the steering of the ship!

For about an hour, while cruising through the Mediterranean at night, I was in full command of our ship. Now, dig this...I was steering backwards while standing looking aft. I had to, in order to reach the wheel and to read the magnetic compass. The quartermaster gave the order, "steer one hundred and fifty seven", and I'd locate that number on the compass. But I had to work just the opposite of what was happening to me and the ship. I was facing aft, so when I wanted to compensate for a swell that would put me to the right of one fifty seven, I'd have to make the adjustment backwards. It was a weird feeling, but after a while, I got into it and was really good at keeping the ship on the nose for over a hundred miles...practically my whole watch. Believe me, I slept fitfully that night. I kept hearing the ocean out there, with all its complicities. I felt powerful.

Mer el Kabir was a name that I would never forget. It was a small town next to Oran, North Africa, where we were docked. It was as if Oran was our home port when we were in the Mediterranean, which was often these days. We certainly didn't object to that! After seven months of action in the English Channel and the Mediterranean Sea, we finally received the order to go home.

The journey home was a joy. Being in the middle of the ocean is exhilarating. There's something about it; the detachment from all that you know, the utter loneliness that is born from that, and the feeling of joy in that loneliness, if that makes sense

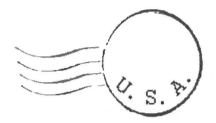

Chapter Eighteen

- - - - - - - - - - - - - - - - -

We returned to the Brooklyn Navy Yard, the place, for me, that it all began. It was a fitting homecoming. What that meant for a lot of men, who had been working hard day and night defending our country. Out of the eight ships in our Destroyer squadron, five had lasted through Normandy. The rest of them had been strewn about all over the Atlantic front. We were very proud of what we had accomplished.

We thought the next assignment was the result of what we'd accomplished, and it would have been, except for the weather. I'd say that this trip checked out our sea worthiness. We were to accompany two new cruisers on their shakedowns. These heavy cruisers, the Pittsburgh and the Springfield, were to take their shakedown in Caribbean waters. They had come down from Boston and we were to join them for the trip further south.

Looking back on the entire experience of life aboard the U.S.S. Murphy, so far, we had been involved in direct warfare, with our guns busy or on alert, doing what Destroyers are supposed to do. Fight. Now it was time for a different sort of life. It was just as important as, say, shooting off our ammunition, but it was certainly less fraught...or so we thought. I think the villain of the piece from here on will be the weather.

Our trip began peacefully enough. The two new cruisers, one heavy, one light, even looked new. That was the first coat of gray primer and somehow it showed. Everything seemed to glisten on board these two ships, as we headed south out of sight of land. Our destination; port of Spain,

Trinidad. Wow! This hayseed hadn't seen anything south of Ocean City in New Jersey.

Before dawn of the second morning out, I came awake as the ground swells had become so huge that I was almost lifted from my bunk, weightless. It sure woke me up, as well as everyone else. We were passing through Cape Hatteras in September, a bad move weather wise. Suddenly it was upon us. I was hardly awake but topside, hanging on for dear life to the life support line that led down to the galley. Soaking wet, I didn't eat much that morning. By noon, we were in the thick of it.

I was on watch in the steering engine room when the exec announced over the PA that the cruisers were in deep trouble. One of them, the Springfield, had come down so heavily from a ground swell that she split in two just forward of the pilot house. There had been adequate warning to evacuate the bow of the ship before she split in two. The old vets on board had seen this Three men were washed overboard and a rescue attempt was being made. Two of them were quickly spotted and somehow taken in on one of the cruisers. The third man appeared nearest to us, so we maneuvered as best we could, and in high seas, to get him closer to the ship, without running him down. The surface of the ocean was now boiling with activity.

Now I seem to remember this very clearly; our ship, just as we got close to the man, bobbed about with engines stopped. This got us in a trough. We rolled more than half way, forty seven degrees on the inclinometer on the galley wall. That meant that the whole port side of the ship submerged and it took another ground swell to right us. During that roll, several of our men were able to reach the man and by the time the roll righted, the man was washed aboard!

We wallowed around for another day waiting for a seagoing tug to arrive and start pulling the Springfield, minus its bow, back to Norfolk. Once south of Hatteras, the voyage turned so sweet that I lay out on the fantail during my watch, and got my first sun tan, with pennies covering my eyes.

The trip into the Gulf Stream was mesmerizing. We all
gathered in the after engine room by the condensers, the
huge copper tanks that constantly circulated ocean water
and through distillation, converted it into fresh water.
That is where we watched the phenomenon of entering the
Gulf Stream. There was a thermometer on the condenser that
kept a record of the water temperature we were entering. It
brought ooh's and aah's as we watched the water temperature
rise dramatically fifteen degrees...and it stayed that way
as long as we were in it.

I was sunburned by the time we reached Port of Spain,
but not enough to dampen my view, though. It was beautiful
in a way I'd never seen before. It was
tropical...completely. We were the only warship in the
harbor. I got liberty and walked into town through a
stretch of jungle. Palm trees of every kind were everywhere
and they were filled with the most exotic birds I had ever
seen. Parrots and Macaws; they all made beautiful noises.

The weather was so warm and humid. I was in heaven again.

I awoke the next morning to a sound that had recently been unheard, that of a shell landing nearby. Racing up to the main deck, I discovered that the noise was far from what I thought it was. Our Warrant Officer, Mr. Soloman, was explaining the ways of the giant manta. That was the noise we had heard; a giant manta ray had flown out of the water. We in came down, it created an explosion with its wings, flapping them against the surface, wanting to attract other fish.

We stayed in the Port of Spain for a week, no longer thinking of war. When we left, we headed north. The trip was uneventful, until we approached Hatteras from the south. Incidentally, we all gathered around the thermometer on the condenser to watch it plummet when we left the Gulf Stream.

By the time we reached Hatteras, another violent storm had started. In fact, it was a hurricane that headed north when we were in Trinidad. Our St. Elmo was working overtime. We ran head on into it. We battened down everything, and in the end, had to abandon the idea of staying topside completely. Within an hour, there was no way to get topside except through the escape hatches. Every time someone opened them, a ton of cold water poured in, drenching those below on the ladder.

At that time it was apparent, due to my fear of shock, that I would never make electrician's mate. So I had become interested in the ships workings and was studying to become a machinists mate. That put me in the after engine room, ironically at the same board that I had nearly sunk the ship at. But in spite of that, I spent a lot of time in that room. I was off duty when the storm struck and decided that the safest place was the after engine room. It was a good decision as we were just aft of being amid ship, the most stable part in a storm. This was no ordinary storm and I spent the night riding it out in that after engine room.

The ship was beyond shuddering. It thudded against each

wave, making your footing dicey, no matter where you were on the ship. In the engine room, we were totally involved with hot machines. The huge diesel engine that ran one of the two forty ton screws at one hundred and forty five thousand horses was next to us, as was the screws axle back to the engine, turning under us. The only machine that wasn't hot was the condenser. Its sides were as cold as the ocean outside. There were meters on all those machines. There were meters all over that room and in conditions like these, had to be read every fifteen minutes. These meters were not conveniently located. A ship only thirty feet wide, had to use every inch of space, and so did we apprentices. My arms were a series of welts brought on by the last pass through the hot maze. My shins, too. But this night, attempts to stand and wriggle through places to read the meters was not a treat; something to get our minds off of what we heard and felt going on outside.

There was a coffee machine in the engine room. We used to say that if we were hit, one of us would immediately start the coffee, because that is barely the time we'd have to enjoy it before we went down. In weather like this, there would be no sense in going up the hatch. Where would you go? Outside? No way...we would stay down here and enjoy one last cup.

By two in the morning we thought it would never end. Not only that, but it sounded and acted like it was increasing as time went on. As we banged into the sea, we were reminded why we were called "tin can sailors". The only separating us from that raging sea was a steel bulkhead only five-eighths of one inch thick. We could hear the ocean out there.

At two thirty that morning we were shocked to hear, and feel, the sound of something as big as a shell, hit the port side with such force that the entire ship shuddered violently. The shuddering never stopped. Something outside in that brutal storm had struck us and then slipped under to hit and damage our screw. We heard the bridge immediately cut down the port screw. Ferguson, one of the old vets who'd been in the engine room off Sicily when a shell came through the board, decapitating his friend, yelled, "I'll make coffee!"...and immediately after that..."Something hit our screw!" He was explaining the violent shuddering of the ship. The exec came over the PA system. "We're okay. We lost the fencing on the port side and it slipped under the ship it was struck by a screw. We'll manage..."

At four in the morning the storm began to ease up and by dawn, a few hours later, the sea was back to normal. We all went up the escape hatch and admired the view. The solid railing had been torn away clear up to the gunwales. We later found that our starboard side twenty six foot whaleboat had been torn from its davit and had vanished. Aside from that, and the damage we already knew about, everything was all right, with the exception of the port screw. The damaged screw insured a wobbly voyage at half speed to Norfolk, where we headed straight into the repair base.

This was my first visit to Norfolk since before I went

aboard my ship. But this was different in that we were in port, and the camp had been inland. Before, I didn't even have a ship and now we were surrounded by ships. We were in Norfolk for about a month and it was getting on into the cold weather of November. We were finally seaworthy. T test the Murphy, we took part in a convoy of merchant ships back to Oran. On that trip, I spotted a periscope. I'd been staring at it, disbelieving what I saw, when the shout came..."Periscope off starboard beam. Three o'clock!" That shout could be heard clear up to the bridge. I had seen it! Then, it disappeared as if it had heard our shouts. An awareness of a whole world under us, swept through the ship. We broke ranks, so to speak, and started circling the area where it had been spotted.

Then came the ash cans. They were rolled off the fantail in twos, the first one set for near surface. Huge plumes startled us, and did more to the submarine sailors, I'm sure. They were now exploding much deeper and raising great humps of water out of the ocean with a deep roar. I found myself empathizing with those submarines. After an hour of this, we gave up circling and sped off toward the convoy. There was no sign that we had bothered the submarine. For the remainder of the trip, we were very aware of the life going on under us in that vast ocean. We managed to get all the ships safely across the Atlantic, and then returned slowly, leisurely.

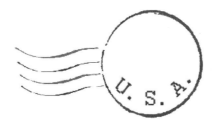

Chapter Nineteen

- - - - - - - - - - - - - - - - -

We really felt like vets when we pulled into the Boston

harbor. It was like entering an old, familiar port. It was

so civilized compared to Norfolk, which seemed to exist

only for the Navy.

So it was to be Christmas in Boston. I remembered last

Christmas, hitchhiking to Rockville Centre from Norfolk,

and getting into that horrific accident at the toll booth.

It was a pleasant Christmas at 22 Norcross Street, the home

of my Aunt Francis and Uncle Russ. This Christmas would be

in a strange city with no relatives. I didn't know anyone

in Boston. I was with two buddies. I can't remember either one of them. It was bitter cold, with the wind blowing the light snow on the ground, as we roamed the streets on Christmas Eve. We had our pea coat collars up and could really feel the cold under the gabardine tailor-mades. For once, I wished I had dressed in my G.I. outfit...all flannel. It had to be warmer than gabardine.

I guess we were a pitiful sight on Christmas Eve, and Boston was a chummy town to us, even though it had this reputation for being uppity. What happened to us belied that description. A car stopped. The window was rolled down and we were invited to Christmas dinner. Just like that. Well, this wasn't behavior exclusively Bostonian, but it was pretty much true, even in Norfolk, that people on the street were kind to servicemen. They were down right concerned for us. (By now, I can imagine a Vietnam vet reading this and rightfully fuming.)

But we went to dinner in a large house in the suburbs. They promised they'd drive us back to the ship. I recall with a slight twinge of disappointment what happened next; we were sitting, all three of us, on the living room sofa. We were talking to the family about where we were from, when one of us, probably drunkenly, dropped his cigarette next to him on the sofa. I didn't smoke, so it wasn't me. I wasn't noticed until one of us smelled it. Instead of showing the burn hole and apologizing for it, one of us quickly moved to the spot and sat on it, hiding the burn hole until after a delicious supper and a pleasant ride back to the ship. I can't remember New Years', but we were all pretty heavy drinkers once we got ashore. Usually well behaved, but prone to let any sailors around us know where we came from. And something unusual, of significance, occurred; a Commodore came on board.

We were elated. For some reason we already knew that we were going to get special attention, regardless of what it was, from now on. Here's the way we heard it would work; a squadron of Destroyers, consisting of eight ships, of around the same class, comes together when there's a special mission at hand. One Destroyer must lead the others, and the one with the Commodore onboard gets to make that decision. This would play a major part in what was about to happen to us.

Within days after the Commodore had settled in...he was a Captain in rank...we became a sealed ship. No one was allowed to go ashore for any reason. All liberties were canceled. We had nothing to do but get the ship ready for a special voyage. Scuttlebutt is a nomenclature word and by now we all know it means rumors are flying. There was mention of our President and scuttlebutt says we are going to be escorting the President someplace, that was all we could gather so far. Okay, now we are going to escort the heavy cruiser, Quincy, someplace. Then, another agonizing day, we put the two together and realized that President Roosevelt was going somewhere on the Quincy and we were going to escort her.

We got underway to Norfolk, where we were to meet up with the Quincy. On the way down, we were briefed by the Commodore. The Quincy, a new heavy cruiser, was to carry

Franklin D. Roosevelt across the sea, destination unknown at the time, but he was going over there for a meeting with all the Allied biggies.

We set off for the Mediterranean on February 1st. We knew that we were going to make this crossing in a hurry. This was nothing like a convoy. There was no slowing down, no stopping along the way, no circling the slow convoy. We raced ahead, our bow faced Africa, and we sped on. Through waves...not over them. At full speed, occasionally reaching flank, speeding along like a knife through the water. The Quincy, riding much like a battleship, moved stealthily through the sea, surrounded by other speeding ships.

Imagine, then, the sight we all held one foggy morning while racing eastward. We were told by the exec over the PA to go up on deck if we were on watch and see the spectacle that was occurring. Rushing topside, we were greeted by the appearance of the Queen Mary, painted as gray as we were, but a giant behemoth rising out of the foggy morning and passing us in the opposite direction at a steady thirty-seven knots, our flank speed and one which we could maintain only sporadically. But here was this giant of a ship, looking out of the fog and passing us all in a matter of five minutes...and at thirty-seven knots! Spectacular! And with a reported four thousand servicemen coming home from the wars. God Speed!

Back to the rigors of maintaining a fast ship. With the Commodore aboard, we had to show the way. We steamed right through the Straits of Gibralter in broad daylight and right on to the tiny islands of Malta once again, stopping there for about a half a day. I can't remember why, but it was a quiet time on Malta, with the engines shut down for the first time since leaving Norfolk. We got there in four days.

Now we were excited, for we heard that we were going to enter the Suez Canal. What impressed us most about the voyage so far was the reflection in the night sky of a fully lit city, that of Cairo, which didn't seem to mind exposing itself. We entered the Canal, one by one, with the

Quincy ahead. Slowly we entered the Canal and sailed down

in perfect weather. It was an awesome sight. I didn't see

it again until I watched "Lawrence of Arabia" in a theatre

in Hollywood, some twenty years later. It's the weirdest

sight, something your eyes must accustom to; the idea of

sailing through water with a desert on both sides. If you

came topside suddenly, you felt the ship was literally

traveling through the desert. It was a sight I'll never

forget.

We came to an opening in the Canal. It was one of the

wide areas of the Canal, the one further down, called

Ismalia. That night, we experienced a phenomenon because

the lights of both Cairo to the south, and Port Saud to the

north, were brightly lit. There was no brownout there. The

combination of a lit sky from the bright city below, and a

night filled with stars combined to make this one of the

most romantic nights imaginable.

I remember going out on deck at night and looking up.

The first thing I saw was Orion's Belt. That constellation

was my favorite, something I picked up on in a Boy Scout camp. I chose the star that represented his heel. That star became the source of communication between me and Joyce Rowland, the girl I had fallen in love with in Rye, New York. I went below and wrote to her that I had been topside and had stared at the star in the constellation that I'd selected. She was to go out on a special night, two weeks from now, and find the star in the constellation. She was to stare at the star for a certain amount of time. I'd be over in the Suez Canal or someplace romantic and we'd be staring at the same star at the same time. It was a romantic gesture that really put me in touch with Joyce. That is what I remember most about Ismalia, the most romantic spot I'd seen so far along my voyage.

We moved slowly down, single file, as the Canal once again became just a canal, being narrow again. Again we were sailing through the desert. Virtually. It was a magic sight. Once again, the Canal opened up and we all come together again, tying up with the Quincy. Once we were there, decisions had to be made. There came word that the

King of Arabia wanted to see the President. But the King had never been out of Arabia before. Whatever ship that would pick up the King and his entourage, would have to be smaller than a Cruiser because the port where we would pick up the King was Jiddah, and no warship of any kind had been in its harbor since World War I...so therefore they had to send a Destroyer. Since the Commodore was aboard my ship, the decision was simple. The voyage would have to be made by us.

As we started, alone, down the rest of the Canal, we were alive with anticipation. The King of Arabia on board a small ship like ours, with an entire entourage, never having been out of the country, precedent had to be established. We kept hearing things over the PA, as the execs would think them. There was to be no eye contact with the King whatsoever. We were to fly the Arabian flag as we entered Jiddah, and our ship would be literally given to the King, along with its crew. The best way to handle this was to assume, while we were on this voyage, that we were all Arabs. Loyal to the King, of course.

The Suez opened up to a natural canal for most of the afternoon. We couldn't get more than half speed because the screws would send waves to both shores. We maintained an even, slow speed until we opened out into the Red Sea. I seem to remember that we had the coast of North Africa off our starboard beam but can't remember whether we saw Arabia until the next day when we entered the port of Jiddah, the "summer Mecca" as it was described to us. Mecca was some miles inland, in the middle of the desert. Jiddah was the largest port on the Red Sea.

When we entered the harbor, we received our first pilot. When any ship, cruise ships and all, enters a port, a pilot comes aboard. It was his responsibility to steer our ship through the harbor and anchor out as close to shore as possible. So imagine the hubbub engendered being not only the sole warship in the harbor, but it was rumored that we were the first steel hulled ship in the harbor since World War I. The pilot took over control of the ship from the skipper, and guided us close to shore and we anchored out.

When the pilot had gotten us as close to shore as possible, we dropped anchor. The pilot left and we were alone, the only warship in port. We got plenty of stares, but we kept busy getting things ready for the King. We knew he hadn't arrived yet because we could see his entourage approaching through the desert. There was a big cloud of dust rising close to the horizon and we were told that it was the caravan of the King, as it approached Jiddah from the east, from Mecca.

The next was amusing and revelatory. The first thing that approached the ship was a barge loaded with thirteen...count 'em...thirteen camels. We wouldn't even let them load one before we adamantly told them that there simply was not room for thirteen camels, that they'd have to turn back. From that moment on, the loading became selective; it was obvious that the King expected something much larger than our little Destroyer, but he was going to have to accept it if he was to meet President Roosevelt.

But, when some ten sheep pulled up alongside, there was a lengthy discussion. The King, it was explained, could only eat meat that had been killed that day by the royal butcher. So both the sheep and the butcher just had to go along, or the King would be deprived of eating.

My beloved fantail...I had grown fond of that position since manning the steering engine room and I just liked the way it felt back there. There was no railing and the stern was always closer to the surface of the ocean than anywhere else on the ship. The ash cans could simply roll right off the side of the ship. It was usually a hang out area. The crew members felt that somehow the rules were eased back aft, and a lot of horseplay went on back there. Sometimes we would tie our laundry to ropes and drag it off the back of the ship. At times like those, you hoped that the ship wouldn't jump into full speed, or you would lose all your clothes.

But not this trip. This trip would have ten sheep roped in and free to roam the fantail...roamimg and waiting to become the next days dinner. The royal butcher announced that he would have to hang that days sheep from the tail mast to clean it. We'd have to belay the union jack that ordinarily hung there.

All told, we also put aboard two steamer trunks that were filled with ten pounds Egyptian notes. The King had never slept under anything but a tent, so a tent was built on board the ship. The barrel in number one five-inch gun up forward was the headliner for the tent. The tent material was brightly colored fabric, regal and magnificent. It was stretched over the gun barrel and secured to the deck on either side. What a sight! A beautiful Arabian tent on the bow and a sheep's carcass waving from the jack staff at the stern.

When the King had come aboard we were all notified of the fact that he couldn't walk. It was rumored that the King had lost the use of his legs during battle, and had to be lifted aboard by a chair in a davit. The entire chair, with the King in it, was lifted on board. The King was immediately taken up forward where he rested under the tent.

But along came his entourage. The King had picked the most famous warrior from each of the territories he had conquered. He was still in the process of unifying Saudi Arabia and it required constant warfare.

The sheiks he had gathered since starting out on this war were certainly warriors, the warriest warriors I have ever seen in seventy five years. In fact, a warrior from one territory was the most beautiful man I have ever seen since then. He was black...I mean black. His skin was the color of charcoal, and of course he wore white, pure white robes that flowed when he walked. He had on two things of color; the two bands that he and the others wore like a crown around their head. He had a scimitar encrusted with gems, including a red ruby. Upon looking at them, I knew that each jewel in that scimitar was real.

Those eyes! I've never seen anything like them since,

their translucent green instantly reminded me of emeralds. The yellow in them, somehow absorbed the color of gold that he wore around his head. Two gems set into deep cobalt. Six feet and three inches, with a dancers' physique, he was as nimble around the rolling deck as a seagoing cat. Between his eyes was a sharp ridge of an ancient Egyptian nose, and below that, a mouth that he somehow had manipulated to remain closed even when he spoke. He spoke clearly in sharp consonants, his language beautiful music from this barren, ancient land. His name, I don't think I ever got. When he opened his mouth, he revealed in a flash, the most exquisite color of white, like a radiant pearl. Let's call him Mohammed.

Mohammed came to the chief machinists mate on the star filled night that we prepped to get underway. With the royal interpreter standing alongside him, he told the chief to look around and to see all those scimitars on all those fearsome Sheiks. There were, I believe, around fifteen of the forty-eight people who ended up being all we could take. (They came with equipment, such as a royal coffee urn, prayer mats, trunks full of money, and the makings of that beautiful tent on the bow of the ship.) Well, the Sheik explained, those scimitars were never to be removed from there scabbards unless it was to defend the bearer. As a consequence, explained the beautiful man, many of them, if not at all, had won their battles a long time ago and because they couldn't extract their scimitars to clean them, they all had been stuck in the scabbards for some time.

That night, under the stars, the machinist's mate and some of the crew, behind closed doors and a growing line outside, took some rust remover and worked Mohammed's scimitar loose. Upon extracting it, they went to work on the blade and handle and all those jewels until the scimitar looked like new. When the others saw the results, they quickly got in line with a promise to do the same for them. I was there. Anyone who was there was sworn to secrecy and we had won over the friendship of everyone of those warriors, including Mohammed. Until now, I've never told anyone of that night. We made friends of some great warriors, and I hope in telling it now that I don't get any of them in trouble.

It took two days to get back to Great Bitter Lake and they were two of the busiest days on board ship. Five times a day, the royal prayer maker would go up to the flying deck and ask which way was Mecca. He then would face it and begin a loud incantation of prayer, at which all forty eight would lay out their prayer rugs on the deck, kneel down and follow the royal prayer makers' chanting.

On the first day out, the royal coffee maker caused a bit of consternation when he was found in the powder room with an open flame, making coffee. We all might have gone up in smoke had he cooked his coffee a little longer. The powder room took on the strange aroma of Turkish coffee, instead of gunnite.

The first night out, the tent shredded. We weren't doing anything more than full speed, and seldom that, but the tent partially flew apart as soon as we headed into the wind. The King just faced the facts and, for the first time in his life, it was said, he went down into the officers' quarters and stayed there the rest of the voyage. He maintained his dignity throughout the trip. We sort of built a throne for him up by the torpedoes. He, obviously, was enjoying himself so far.

From his throne, he was able to watch, along with all of us, as we showed a film, "Battle of Midway", on the foredeck; something we had done about a half a dozen times on our voyages. The King was unimpressed with all the war material in the film. At least that was the word we got from the gunnery officer.

As we approached the Suez, the King wanted to meet everyone on the ship to thank us. He gave the officers each a scimitar, complete with jewels and scabbard. To each of us non-commission crew; we were lined up on the superstructure and then went up and shook his hand. I can't recall whether he gave us the notes himself, or if he had someone else do it. That seemed to be the case because it was the purser that said the notes were worth forty one dollars and thirty eight cents but we could opt to keep the notes as souvenirs. I chose to keep the new note, for the time being anyway.

When we arrived at Great Bitter Lake, we tied up to the Quincy. Keep in mind that on our fantail, we were about a deck from the ocean. It was about six feet between us standing on the fantail and the sea. When we tied up to something as big as a Cruiser, or the last time, an Aircraft Carrier, we were tying up to a ship that stood four of five decks at the stern, or as much as forty or fifty feet from the oceans surface.

So it was that, on our first morning back at Great Bitter Lake, I was working at the stern as usual, putting things in order, swabbing the deck, making the necessary adjustments while we were standing still, when from the deck of the Quincy, high above us, we heard a familiar voice. It was the President himself. He wheeled his chair over to the side looking down on our deck. The President clearly said, "Nice looking ship you have there, boys!" To which several of us responded immediately, "Thank you, sir!" He turned in his chair and was gone, wheeling himself away from the gunwale.

Getting the King on board the Quincy was pretty simple; they used the same chair lift that was used to put President Roosevelt on board. To this day, I remember the Kings full name, even though I might misspell part of it; Abdul Assiz Ibn Abdul Rahman Al Faisal Al Saud...there. It was rumored that he had fifty two sons and an unknown amount of daughters, as females didn't count. Only four of his sons were primed for royalty. One, it turns out, the son that eventually took over as King, was an Oxford graduate. He was a fascinating man.

Pvt. Tom Black Joins Two Rye Buddies In Final Sleep On Bloody Iwo Jima

FIFTH MARINE DIVISION

IN GRAVE 713, ROW 6, PLOT 3, of this Fifth Marine Division Cemetery on Iwo Jima, rests Pvt. Thomas M. Black, son of Mr. and Mrs. William T. Black, 396 Midland Avenue, Rye, who gave his life, along with many other leathernecks, in the performance of his duty to his country. In the background rises Mt. Suribachi. The flag flies at half staff out of respect to the late President Roosevelt.

—AP Photo

My cousin Russel, We shared Morse codes together in Italy.

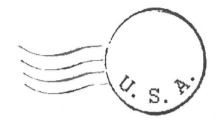

Chapter Twenty

- - - - - - - - - - - - - - - - -

Since I was striking for machinist mate. I was given the diesel engine in the whaleboat to maintain, much as I had been in charge of batteries when I was an electrician. Since there was only one whaleboat, the other having been lost at Hatteras and not replaced in Norfolk, only the starboard side whaleboat was available. So it was, around the fifteenth of February, that I and the twenty six foot whaleboat were called into service.

It was a beautiful, romantic night with the glow of Cairo visible in the night sky, filled with stars. Great

Bitter Lake was as serene as it was glassy, as I started up the diesel and we lowered into placid waters. With the diesel chugging, I was below deck. That is, there was an awning like structure over the bow where the engine and I were. It opened aft where I could spot the legs of the quartermaster as he stood by the stern, holding the rudder. We pulled up to a pier and I threw it into reverse. I cannot remember now whether or not we knew who we took on board for the trip out to the Quincy, but I recall we all assumed it was Churchill. The reason being that although I was in the dark, under the canopy, not able to see clearly in the dark, illuminated by stars, just whom we had on board. But, I distinctly recall that I smelled cigar smoke. That is what clenched it for me. I just assumed that the only person who'd be smoking a cigar at this time of night, it was nearly midnight...it must have been Churchill. But looking back on it, I don't think that as important a person as Churchill would have been treated this way. But who knows? If Churchill was there, and that can be proven, then I was in the same whaleboat, although I didn't have a conversation with him. Only with Roosevelt!

The next day was my birthday. As we completed our mission and sailed on up through the Suez Canal and out into the Mediterranean, I celebrated my nineteenth birthday. Wow! Thanks to the Navy, I had been involved in the invasion of Normandy, and southern France, had chased the Graf Spee, had gunboat encounters with Germans at Cherbourg and at Corsica. I had been dive bombed by Germans, had vacationed off the southern coast of France, including San Tropez, had visited Naples, seen Mt. Etna doing its thing, etcetera, etcetera, and on the seventeenth of February, I turned nineteen years of age...quite a beginning of life for a wanderer off the farm.

We sailed back to New York for a short stay in the ship yard. Our heads were still spinning from the voyage out of the Arabian Nights. Literally. We were not prepared for the next tour of duty. It seemed that we were being put out to pasture, was how the exec described it.

It was nearing the end of the war in Europe. (To us it

was the only war.) There were a bunch of German submarines that were operating out of the Bay of Fundy, between Newfoundland and Nova Scotia. They would patrol the east coast, sinking Liberty ships as they exited New York harbor or Boston harbor, or Philadelphia. That would give them the propaganda lift they needed. In order to stay along the east coast and not have to return to Germany each time they ran out of fuel or ammunition, they had at least one mother ship up in the Bay of Fundy. They would go up there for refueling, etc., and we were to trap them up in the Bay and sink them, one by one. We weren't sure just how many there were up there at any given time but we had plans to trap them in the Bay and we were to be part of that trap.

We were to form a line of Destroyers along the bottom of the Bay, thereby trapping any subs in the Bay. They would have to get through us to get back to Germany. We hadn't counted on the weather. We thought it didn't get much colder than Boston or Portland, Maine, until we got up into the Bay of Fundy.

I look at the Bay of Fundy as one big freezer. Of course, there was no frozen food back then but in retrospect, that was the experience I came away with. It was bone chilling cold all the time. And what was odd about the weather was the fog. I couldn't understand how the fog, which was thick at some times, could hang around in below zero weather. But it did. For days, nay, for weeks, we patrolled the line while enveloped in fog so thick you couldn't see the bow from the pilot house, and it was twenty below. This turned out to be the longest voyage without seeing land for fifty four days, the longest we were ever at sea.

On April twelfth, we received sad news, as did the rest of the world. Franklin D. Roosevelt, the President of the United States, had died at his retreat in Warm Springs, Va or Ga, I'm not sure.

The entire ship went into mourning. Any conversation had to do with his death, but mostly the crew was quiet, a quiet ship. I was deeply saddened. I wrote a long letter about what a good person he was and how he hung in there until practically the last moment...courageously. He would be solely missed by the entire world. I felt as if the war had come to a stop this day, and it would within a month.

We had two encounters. Both were detected by sonar. We rolled ash cans off the fantail and blew them into the air from the side guns we had under the ash cans, so they'd fly up and out about twenty yards from the ship. We dropped them at various depths and saw debris start to surface. That was enough for us. We didn't think during these moments that there would be any survivors. It was just assumed that once hit, that was it. There would be no way out. It wasn't a pleasant experience. Several of us jumped up and down when the debris showed up, but that quickly stopped and the rest of the excitement centered on what the flotsam consisted of. When we saw that they had bunks like ours, it took the kick away. It became more personal, like letting our wildest nightmare come true. We were a somber lot all through this duty.

We finally came into port for refueling. I don't remember where it was, but it was up in Nova Scotia. There was no relief, at that time, from the cold. Except for one special place...

My favorite hangout on the ship was just behind the forward stack. There were two slabbed-sided, slightly racked stacks. The rear stack carried the Shamrock that we had put up there after Normandy. Each stack had a skirt around its base. Under the skirt, hot air rushed out as a means of getting the smoke to rise fast through and out the stacks. The result of this action was to shoot hot air from under the skirts at the base of the stacks. They were of such size that you could, while standing up, lean back and let the upper body rest against the side of the stack while under you, around your knees, came this wonderful, life saving hot air.

It was fabulous. You could be at flank speed through this icy sea and still feel warm as toast. It was a great feeling. You felt invincible. Someone always brought a big, steaming pot of "Navy coffee", famous for its strength. It was heaven to stand leaning against the stack, hot air billowing up under your dungarees, while someone from the galley poured you a steaming hot cup of java. No where was this more appreciated than during the Bay of Fundy tour. I think the total count of that operation was seven, although by that time a lot of U boats were pulling into local ports and surrendering.

Back in Boston, after a chilling trek, I was instantly warmed up by a letter that was waiting for me. It was a letter from Mr. Clarke, the principal of Williamstown High School. He invited me back to Williamstown for high school graduation!

I had attended Williamstown for two years. At that time the educational system in the country went through dramatic changes during the war. Williamstown was in farm country and that was definitely important at the time. I and practically every man in my junior class would be exempt from going off to war if he so desired. That was because we, in my class, were all Future Farmers of America. We wore jackets with 'colors' describing us as such.

After the regular school courses in the morning, we'd spend the afternoons in Mr. Carrolls' agricultural class. One day a week we would go up to Ed Wynns' garage and become mechanics. We'd actually get down under the car needing service, and in some cases, we'd service them. We were kept busy all day at Ed Wynns' garage, The girls of course were doing Home Economics. On week-ends we would go as groups to the Fairs and judge the live stock. I got really good at judging cattle and to this day can recognize a good milker when I see one.

Looking back, I'd say the curriculum was pretty good and practical. I feel that I learned more from those aggie courses than most other subjects. But I wanted to join the Navy, so I left Williamstown and hitchhiked to Rye, New York, in search of my big adventure. While attending Rye High School, I enlisted with my buddies, and then settled in to wait for the Navy to call.

And now Williamstown was offering me a graduation! With my record of achievement in the Navy, the school decided that I was eligible. The only trouble was, when I got to Boston, I was broke. (I can honestly say that I don't remember how much we were paid or when we were paid or how we ever cashed our checks.) To get there would require a train ride from Boston to Williamstown, a trip clear across the state of Massachusetts. I got permission from the executive officer for leave to go but where was I to come up with the money?

I remembered the ten pound Egyptian note and what it was worth. Forty one dollars and thirty eight cents. That would certainly get me there. I went into Boston on my first liberty and entered a bank. I easily obtained the money and got the train. You could say, and I have on occasion, that the King of Arabia financed my graduation from high school. And why not? He was a personal friend. After all, hadn't I shaken his hand and didn't he give me that money as a gift?

So I graduated. There were forty five in the graduating class and there were three of us in the service who were graduating in uniform. It was quite a thrill, being looked upon as a hero as well as a graduate. But I discovered, most of the people I'd run into on this leave, were shocked to see me. One woman actually broke down in tears. I finally put it all together and it was the Shamrocks that were responsible.

During the invasion of Normandy, we were not allowed to hang our giant Shamrocks on the after stack. But as soon as we got back to England, and before the bombardment of Cherbourg, we stuck them proudly back on. So when we were racing around the English Channel, trying to avoid the sixteen-inch shells that were whooshing over us, we were flying the Shamrocks.

The Germans loved specific identifications. Once they determined that it was the U.S.S. Murphy out there lobbing five-inch shells at them, the jig was up. They sent word around the world that one of the ships hit and sunk, with all hands on board, had been the mighty Murphy! Of course, we didn't know that but several of the townspeople did. It was something of an eerie event. My graduation was bittersweet. It was beautiful, and at the same time I realized that I probably would not return to Williamstown and the Future Farmers of America. After all, I was an adventurer now and had much more of the world to conquer...much more than Williamstown could offer.

I returned to Boston and we were sent immediately on a convoy. It was to be our last crossing of the Atlantic. It was off our home base in the Mediterranean once more, taking a bunch of Liberty ships to that North African port, Oran, one that was familiar to us all.

It was an uneventful crossing but a historical stay. On May 8th, 1945, we were in Mers el Kebir, which is the harbor of Oran. We were all gathered around the radio in the bowels of the ship, when it was announced...the war, our war, was over! Germany had surrendered Hitler was dead in his bunker. The Russians were marching into Berlin and it was all over. We had won!

For the first time, on our way back to Boston, the Pacific became the topic of conversation. We were sure that we'd win the war now. It would be good to get some Pacific time in, although that was far from us and as always we thought of it as "the other war". I couldn't seem to get into the idea of going west.

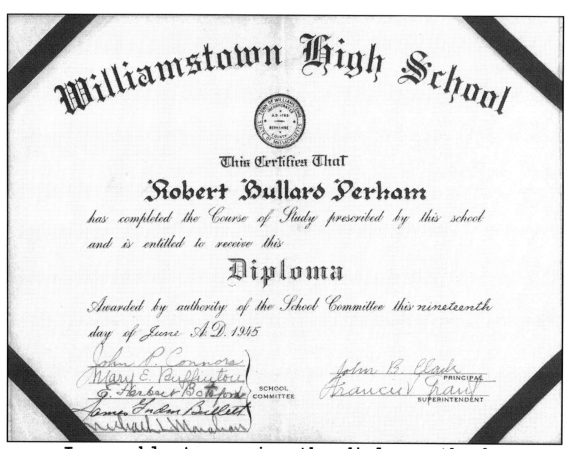

I was able to receive the diploma, thanks
to the King of Arabia.

GRADUATION EXERCISES

WILLIAMSTOWN HIGH SCHOOL

WILLIAMSTOWN, MASSACHUSETTS

0 194

at 8 o'clock

in the

ADAMS MEMORIAL THEATRE

Williamstown High School graduation poster.

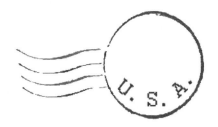

Chapter Twenty-One

- - - - - - - - - - - - - - - - - -

Back in Boston, I seemed to have come full circle. I felt that especially when I was notified by the exec that several of us were being transferred off the ship. Oddly enough, I don't remember one reason given for it. Looking back on it, there must have been some discussion of it before Boston.

At that point, I was tired. As a wanderer all my life, I know and relish that kind of tired. It means that I've gotten everything I could out of this experience and now it was time to move onto another. Of course, that wasn't the reasoning at that time. I don't remember the feelings of that time, but I recall that leaving the ship was not as dramatic as boarding it for the first time. I think I might have felt that the war was nearly over, that the Pacific and the Japanese were another war, a war I knew I wasn't interested in. I guess by then I'd had mine. We won. That was that.

That was that. I shipped off on a train for Norfolk. I don't remember the train ride at all. But I do remember things about Norfolk. It started one night in August. It was hot and muggy, even on the ferry taking me across the bay from the base to the city, and particularly in Norfolk. Norfolk was not exclusively Navy. There were soldiers all around, waiting for ships to take them on their next tour of duty. It was a bustling military town. I hooked up with three soldiers for a night of heavy drinking, mainly Southern Comfort. Something I have never drunk since.

I got awfully drunk, as did all of us, and one soldier, an admittedly rich soldier, got us a room in a hotel in

Norfolk. I must have passed out, because the next thing I remember is waking up with this soldier in bed with me, kissing me and trying to have sex with me. This was my first homosexual encounter and I wasn't ready for it. I fought my way out of bed, got dressed and, still feeling the effects of the Southern Comfort, staggered out of the hotel, feeling disgusted and filthy. I found my way to the ferry boat and once aboard, read the morning paper. I was very close to throwing up. It was the first and only time I ever felt seasick.

On the cover of the newspaper was a picture of what looked like a giant mushroom. It became apparent that it was a mushroom cloud from an explosion. The headlines read: "ATOMIC BOMB DROPPED ON HIROSHIMA". It was all so confusing. What was an atomic bomb? My head was spinning and I could still smell the soldiers all over me. I tried to read the article but I couldn't focus through my nausea.

The consequences from that bomb estimated four hundred thousand people dead in one explosion, one bomb. It seemed that the war up until now had meant nothing. It was as if we had been fighting with old fashioned weapons. Now the war had escalated to new heights. New, horrible heights.

When I staggered off the ferry that morning in early August, I was sure the war was over. Even the papers said so. Japan must surrender with this new deadly bomb. It seemed I hadn't got over the first bomb when the second, at Nagasaki, was dropped. Japan immediately surrendered. On August 5th, the news came officially. The war was over.

The streets of Norfolk became hysterical. I even bolted from the base, along with many others, and ran down the street, proclaiming victory. Now that I look back on it, Norfolk was a pretty sad town to be in on such an occasion, but what the hell, it was over!

I couldn't help worrying about the Murphy and its crew. I knew it was on its way to Japan. They had sailed down from Boston and cruised through Norfolk one day on their way to the Canal. I went on board and they told me that they were heading for Japan. I was glad that I wasn't going with them.

I got orders that I was to be transferred to San Diego, California. I boarded a troop train in Norfolk, Virginia, and spent eleven days entering a new adventure. Three of those eleven days were spent going through Texas. It was late August. It was hot and muggy the entire trip. We sweated across the country, and I distinctly remember the conductor saying, "You could look ahead three days and see nothing but Texas." I was impressed on how big the State was.

Yes, we had conductors on the cattle cars, one conductor for each car. And they were dressed just like conductors. The one we had was particularly kind and helpful. He was a black man with much of the same features as my Arab friend, but he was much older. He was of a reedy build but held himself upright and was as neat a conductor as I've ever seen. How he managed to keep so cool and neat in this weather with the cars reeking and dusty, was beyond me. A troop train consisted of cattle cars with bunk beds, three high and bolted to the floor of each car. The bunks were not claimable. This meant that as night approached, you got into a bunk and stayed there or lost your bunk. Then you would have to sleep on the floor between the cars or near the break.

A favorite spot on the trip was between the cars because it was the coolest place. The cars reeked of cattle, making us all smell more like cows than sailors. I should have felt right at home, having come from the farm. On the fourth or fifth day out, I lost all the bunks and slept in the space between cars. It was cooler at night for sleeping, anyway, and I actually preferred to sleep on the floor.

I was asleep on the floor when I awoke feeling something unusual was happening. I didn't move, but slowly opened my eyes under my hat, which I had placed over my eyes while sleeping. The conductor had unbuttoned the flap on my pants and was deftly reaching into my pants and very gently pulled my penis out and leaning forward, gently sucked my already hard penis. I was so amazed by this behavior, with other sailors lying by and with enough light to see him. I had the wherewithal to remain quiet and faking asleep right through my orgasm, after which the conductor gently put my penis back and buttoned me up. It was one of the most bizarre events that took place while I was in the Navy and at the time convinced me that I must be doing something that attracts other men. I couldn't figure out what it was. It certainly wasn't intentional. But for a nineteen year old, it was just one more item on my long list of things happening to me during the war.

Another was to be in California for the first time. I really felt it viscerally. I think it was the weather. And back in those days, California, especially southern California, featured so many orange groves. It was September and the smell of blooming orange blossoms filled the air. It was beautiful, more beautiful than any perfume I'd ever smelled. "Those are the Valencias", said my conductor.

From San Diego, we were bussed down to National City, which was described as the nearest city to Mexico, just above the boarder from famed Tijuana. The base, the U.S. Naval Destroyer Repair Base, was best described as scruffy. It was, like so much of California I'd experienced so far, constantly dusty, a hot dryness that I hadn't felt before. It was good, a little like Oran.

The base was situated on both sides of the main highway that led along the coast from Los Angeles, I was told, all the way down to Tijuana. The east side of the road housed all the barracks and was kept pretty clean. On the ocean side, it was a different matter. That was where, by now, the ships were pouring in every day, loaded down with Army and Marines home from the war.

At the time, since before we left Norfolk, almost as soon as the war in Europe had ended, a point system was worked out that determined just when you were going to be discharged. I don't remember how the points were determined, but shortly after I arrived in San Diego, I was able to figure out just when I'd be discharged...somewhere in March.

Two things happened while I was at the base that I remember; one was a visit to the base from the U.S.S. Murphy. I managed to catch a barge out to the anchored ship and spent a morning on board with the crew. There I learned that the Murphy was the fourth ship into Nagasaki harbor after it was bombed. The scene was one of horror. It was obvious when they sailed into the port that the war was over. No country could feel safe anymore with that bomb in existence. It was unimaginable, what they saw, and smelled. The smell said it all. It was awful, the smell of hundreds of thousands of bodies still there, with no one there to clean up afterward. It was simply the end of the war as we know it. And none of the crew liked it. By then, we all knew the horrors of the bomb. I've wondered ever since if my luck hadn't been with me when I transferred off the ship. I'd like to see the record of cancer among the crew members who were so fast to enter that harbor after the bomb.

I had about two months before discharge. What to do with my time? I was very fond of music and had been way before I saw Duke Ellington at my high school. When I went into the Navy, I had already amassed several scrapbooks filled with items for Metronome and Downbeat, and stories about some of my favorites. I was about to experience first hand a lot of what I'd only been reading about. In fact, I was about to hear some.

San Diego was a good, clean city with fresh, warm air wafting through, boosted along by a constant on shore breeze. The beach area downtown was mostly off limits to non-coms. The Coronado, for instance, was already a famous name, but it was known strictly as a Naval pilots hangout, not a lowly first class seaman. So I don't remember ever being in the Coronado. But everywhere else. It was all new and exciting to me. I struck up a friendship with a nurses' aid who lived up the hill by the big Navy hospital. She was a sweet young thing and was wildly sensual. She was younger

that I thought, seventeen, and I was an old man, just about
to celebrate my twentieth birthday. We decided to spend my
birthday together, really together. We'd get a room in a
hotel. We chose the Golden West Hotel in the center of
town.

One thing I learned about when entering California;
there was a terrible fear of earthquakes. You heard about
it all the time. If that wasn't enough, there were several
laws in effect which caused a constant awareness. The most
prominent law was the one that stated no building in the
state of California could be over thirteen stories high.
Thus, the El Cortez, a white Spanish style hotel up the
hill, was at thirteen stories. It was the highest building
in San Diego, which is what gave the city, and all others
in California, I was to discover, such a feeling of
openness. With this weather, it was some combination.

The Golden West Hotel was a big building. I can't
remember how tall. I walked in alone and asked for a room.
It was on one of the upper floors. The plan was for her to

come in the side entrance about five minutes after I'd gone in and got the room. After I registered, I walked outside to tell her the room number, then walked into the main lobby and took the elevator up. She waited five minutes and then came up the stairs from the side entrance.

I was breathing heavily with anticipation when there was a gentle knock on the door. I opened it and she came in, smiling nervously. We embraced, and, like two conspiring friends, we started undressing. I got my flap down and got her silk stockings just about off, lying there on the bed, when there came a strident knocking on the door.

In a panic, she started rolling her stockings up her legs again and I hastily pulled my pants up and started buttoning as a voice on the other side of the door said loudly, with another, more deliberate pounding of the door, "Vacate this room immediately and turn your keys in downstairs", came the booming command.

Needless to say, we were terrified. She was near tears as we embraced for a final time and she went down the way she'd come up. I had to go down to the desk. As I left the key and started the long walk through the lobby, I heard throughout the lobby, "Don't you ever come to this hotel again...and so young." Since I was the only sailor in the hotel at the time, it wasn't hard to pick me out. I was mortified. That sort of ended the romance. Besides, she had a job and I was anxious to start hearing some music. Now let's see how much I remember:

There was the Pacific Ballroom at the north end of San Diego. There was the Mission Beach Ballroom up north along the shore. I would hitch-hike up to Los Angeles to see bands at the Palladium and one other big ballroom in the city. When I hitch-hiked to Los Angeles, there were towns on the outskirts of the city which provided housing for servicemen. There was a very popular place in Huntington Park, which became my home away from home. It was called the Huntington Park Hospitality House. It was a house converted into a bed and breakfast of sorts, where I could get a clean bunk and be provided with some great food when I'd come wandering in drunk and hungry after a night of dancing to some of the great bands. The Huntington Park Hospitality House had made a deal with local churches and had weddings on the week-ends. They would gather all the left over food and deliver it to us. I dined on shrimp and crab, all sorts of stuff that I'd never even heard of. It was a wonderful place, full of good memories.

The Southgate Ballroom was close by and Lionel Hampton was there. He was fabulous and the band awesome. Their most popular song at the time and a hit all over the country, was "Hey Bobareebop", something every sailor that I saw was humming. That was the ballroom that I frequented most often. I usually arrived back at the Hospitality House soaking wet with sweat from four or five hours of non-stop dancing.

If it wasn't Lionel Hampton, it was Les Brown at the Palladium with Doris Day singing "Sentimental Journey" and others. Stan Kenton followed Les Brown into the Palladium and June Christy was singing, "Willow Weep For Me" and "Across The Alley From The Alamo, Lived A Pinto Pony And A Navajo..."

It wasn't bad getting caught in San Diego, either. At the Pacific Ballroom were Gene Krupa and Anita O'Day belting out "Trav'lin Light". There was a small club in San Diego which featured Sara Vaughan, an up and coming blues singer. Meanwhile, up in Los Angeles, the Brown Derby featured Red Nichols and his Five Pennies. The swinging sounds of Benny Goodman came from the Mission Beach Ballroom, featuring Helen Ward and Art Lund. I particularly liked the arrangements by the Goodman band. So there was lots to do and hear during those months in California.

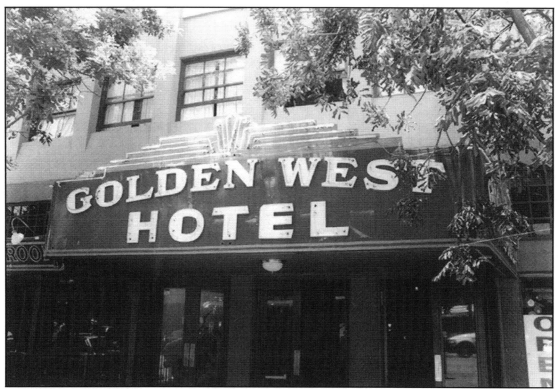

The Golden West Hotel, San Diego, California.

Hotel lobby.

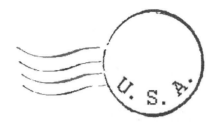

Chapter Twenty-Two

— — — — — — — — — — — — — — —

There was also a phenomenon happening at the Naval
Repair base. At the end of every pier in the Naval Repair
base, was a pile of clothes. Not just clothes, but new
clothes, still bound in bales. Ten pairs of heavy woolen
socks, baled together. Bales of dungarees, chambray shirts,
hundreds of Kapok jackets that we wore at sea all the time.
Rapidly, these mounds of clothes became, over a period of
just a few days, a mountain of clothing. Each ship that
came into port emptied itself of every bit of extra
clothing aboard.

The mountains grew big, some forty to fifty feet across and over ten feet in height, and along about the fifth day all were set on fire! For weeks, all we could smell throughout the base was burning clothes, brand new clothes. The reason given that if these clothes were all suddenly appearing in the Army-Navy stores, it would hurt the economy.

The postwar economy was going strong, and a bunch of freebees thrown on the market would stall it. So several of us went down and salvaged some clothes to send home. I got a couple of jackets and a big pair of Army ski boots that were, in fact, gigantic boots. I wore them all through college later on, often using them for skiing.

Back in those days your boots didn't have to fit the skis but were strapped on with six foot lengths of leather, literally tying you to the skis. It was a wonder that I didn't break every bone in my legs. We were caught and threatened by the MP's. But we collected the clothes anyway and sent them home.

I took up writing my first short story. It was about Johnny Naughton, a fellow sailor from New York City who wanted to become a New York City Policeman. With his thick New York accent, he used to call me "Robit". The story was about a USO show that we'd seen together. I had asked several of my friends to read and critic the piece, including Johnny Naughton. I was relieved and excited that they liked it. I guess, from then on, I considered myself a writer. By March 10th, I had accumulated enough points to be discharged.

It had been one hell of a ride for a hayseed from Vermont, barely twenty years old. To top things off and make this voyage complete, I was informed that I would, indeed, get Pacific duty before I retired.

They sent us to San Pedro, outside of the Los Angeles harbor, some three hundred miles up the coast by ship. We were to sail up to San Pedro on a Destroyer Escort. That was a ship who's nomenclature I failed to mention...because we tin soldiers had disdain for them. The very name aroused ire. What Destroyer needs an "escort"? They were slow, cumbersome vessels with one five-inch gun located up on the bow, which looked pretty silly. Anyway, they took about fifty of us this day. We rode all the way topside on a glorious, sun-filled morning. There we were, dressed in our blues and enjoying ourselves while we served our Pacific duty. We were all happy and in good spirits. After all, we were about to be discharged. It was Thursday.

Our cruise lasted from 10:00 a.m. To about 5:00 p.m. Terminal Island was a welcomed sight. San Pedro harbor was pretty organized. It had to be with the numbers of servicemen that were coming through every day. This is where we were to be processed, the place where we would find our freedom. They had a system, and we fell right into it.

We were given our quarters for the next few days. Next, we had a hearty dinner in the large mess hall. The anticipation of the following days' events, had us all a little giddy.

The next day, Friday, we set out to gather our papers and start the process of discharge. Among other things, I was given an accounting of my service that would show on my honorable discharge. A Lieutenant in charge of filling out documents, began to drill me. "Let's see, what do you plan to do upon discharge?" Then I was back on the farm, I had been interested in becoming a Veterinarian and had thought about attending Cornell University, as they had a good Vet's course. I then remembered the writer in me and those few short stories that I had written at the Repair base in National City. After all, they had been enjoyed by my cohorts. That inspired me. So I told the officer, and he wrote, "Journalism" in the proper space.

The Lieutenant began again. "Let's see, you were involved in the invasion of Normandy, the bombardment of Cherbourg, and the invasion of southern France. So that gives you three battle stars on your European Conflict ribbon." I then asked, "What about the Good Conduct medal?"

Receiving the Good Conduct medal required you to spend three years of clean duty. My three years would be up in three days, on Monday. As I brought this to his attention, he suggested that I hang around the base for the week-end. I could pick up my medal on Monday. It didn't take long for me to reply, "No thanks. I'm out of here!" With that I signed my discharge papers. I wanted to spend the week-end free.

The following day was Saturday and it was pouring rain. I gathered up all my belongings and received my Ruptured Duck pin (a pin that you were to wear on your uniform which states that you've been discharged). At about four o'clock in the afternoon, with me sea bag over my shoulder, I stepped off the curb and put up my thumb. It was still pouring rain.

Thus ended three years of excitement in my life. I hadn't been twenty years old for more than a month, and I sure got started on a road to adventure. And now, I was

beginning a brand new one; my trip back to the East Coast.
I had chosen to be discharged in Los Angeles so that I
could hitch-hike across the country.

My first ride was with a man in a car. When I told him
my plans, he thought I was crazy. "Why don't you fly home?
There are troop planes flying in and out of Long Beach
every day. Why don't you hitch a ride with them?"

As I sat there, sopping wet already, I reconsidered. He
drove me to the airfield in Long Beach and wished me luck.
After waiting an hour, a plane came in. A Sergeant Major
got off the plane and began sloshing through the water to
the terminal. As he passed me I said, "I'm heading for New
York. Can you help me?" After sizing up my wet rat
condition he replied, "I've got forty soldiers on that
plane and forty one seats. Get on!" I picked up my sea bag
and started wading towards the plane.

When I entered the plane I saw forty Army soldiers
sitting in the bucket seats that were lined up against the

side walls of the interior. I was the only sailor. Someone from the far end rang out, "Up here sailor". I had to walk through a lot of them to find my seat at the very end of the plane.

We flew to Dallas and landed to refuel. While we were there, a Sergeant came on board. Spying me he said, "What are you doing here? Get off right now." At this point, the soldiers raised a stink. "What do ya mean? Let him stay, he's all wet." The officer was out numbered and left the plane. So we were off to Newark, New Jersey. Upon arrival I hitched a ride into New York City, which was easy for any serviceman at the time. From Times Square I took the subway, costing me a dime, to Greenwich Village where my grandmother Perham lived. She was so surprised when she opened her door and saw me standing there. I dropped my bag and gave her a hug. "Hi Grandma, I'm home."

So I made it home in nineteen hours and fifty minutes, hitch-hiking from San Pedro to Greenwich Village. And it only cost me ten cents!

The End

He Made a Slight Correction

A POST-WAR ANECDOTE

WHILE our destroyer was hugging the shore of Omaha Beach during the invasion of Normandy, we were constantly on the alert for enemy planes. The morning of D Day plus two, during a lull in the action, we members of the black gang were enjoying the sun topside when suddenly over the public-address system the executive officer's voice warned us, "Six planes in vicinity. Six planes in vicinity."

As usual, we disbanded and shuffled off for the engine room and fireroom hatches, fully expecting bombs and confusion. But just as we got to our positions, the exec's voice again boomed out, "Friendly planes. Friendly planes." So we filed back into the sunlight and relaxed again, doing no worrying about the six planes now droning high above our ship.

A few minutes later, five or six terrific explosions ripped the water front, and our ship rocked violently as we got the full force of the concussion. Stunned, we hesitated a couple of seconds, and then—as the deafening "clang, clang, clang" of GQ sounded—went diving down the hatches to our battle stations.

At that moment, amid the clamor and confusion, the exec once more spoke over the PA system. In a somewhat embarrassed, apologetic voice he announced, "Friendly bombs. Friendly bombs."

—ROBERT PERHAM.

NOTICE OF SEPARATION FROM U. S. NAVAL SERVICE

NAVPERS-553 (REV. 9-45)

1. SERIAL OR FILE NO. 2. NAME (LAST) (FIRST) (MIDDLE) 3. RATE AND CLASS OR RATING AND CLASSIFICATION 4. PERMANENT ADDRESS FOR MAILING PURPOSES	5. PLACE OF SEPARATION
710-90-34 PERHAM, Robert Bullard Fireman, First Class (EM) USNR V-6 223 Oakland Beach Ave. Rye, New York Westchester County	PSC NB TI SAN PEDRO, CALIF.

				6. CHARACTER OF SEPARATION
				HONORABLE
				7. ADDRESS FROM WHICH EMPLOYMENT WILL BE SOUGHT
				Same as #4

8. RACE	9. SEX	10. MARITAL STATUS	11. U.S. CITIZEN (YES OR NO)	12. DATE AND PLACE OF BIRTH
White	Male	Single	Yes	2-17-26 Atlantic Co. Margate, New Jersey

13. REGISTERED	14. SELECTIVE SERVICE BOARD OF REGISTRATION	15. HOME ADDRESS AT TIME OF ENTRY INTO SERVICE
YES ☐ NO ☒	None	Rye, New York

16. MEANS OF ENTRY (INDICATE BY CHECK IN APPROPRIATE BOX)	17. DATE OF ENTRY INTO ACTIVE SERVICE	18. NET SERVICE (FOR PAY PURPOSES) (YRS., MOS., DAYS)
☒ ENLISTED ☐ INDUCTED ☐ COMMISSIONED 3-19-43 DATE	3-19-43	02-11-28

19. PLACE OF ENTRY INTO ACTIVE SERVICE
New York, New York

20. QUALIFICATIONS, CERTIFICATES HELD, ETC.	21. RATINGS HELD	22. FOREIGN AND/OR SEA SERVICE WORLD WAR II
See rating booklet #15264 Fireman, First Class	AS, S2c, F3o(EM), F2c(EM), F1o(EM)	☒ YES ☐ NO

23. SERVICE SCHOOLS COMPLETED	WEEKS	24. SERVICE (VESSELS AND STATIONS SERVED ON)
EM School, Great Lakes, Ill.	16	USS MURPHY (DD-603) Ind Com., USNRB, San Diego, Calif.

IMPORTANT: IF PREMIUM IS NOT PAID WHEN DUE OR WITHIN THIRTY-ONE DAYS THEREAFTER, INSURANCE WILL LAPSE. MAKE CHECKS OR MONEY ORDERS PAYABLE TO THE TREASURER OF THE U. S. AND FORWARD TO COLLECTOR'S SUBDIVISION, VETERAN'S ADMINISTRATION.   346 Broadway N.Y. 13, N.Y.

25. KIND OF INSURANCE	26. EFFECTIVE MONTH OF ALLOTMENT DISCONTINUANCE	27. MO. NEXT PREMIUM DUE	28. AMOUNT OF PREMIUM DUE EACH MONTH	29. INTENTION OF VETERAN TO CONTINUE INS.
NSI	3-46	4-46	6.40	Yes

30. TOTAL PAYMENT UPON DISCHARGE	31. TRAVEL OR MILEAGE ALLOWANCE INCLUDED IN TOTAL PAYMENT	32. INITIAL MUSTERING OUT PAY	33. NAME OF DISBURSING OFFICER
$ 187.03	$ 155.55	$100.	Lt. G. L. OWEN (SC) USN

34. REMARKS	35. SIGNATURE (BY DIRECTION OF COMMANDING OFFICER)
Point System American Area European-African Area, 3 Stars Victory Medal World War II	*[signature]* J. B. WARNER, Lt. Comdr., USNR

36. NAME AND ADDRESS OF LAST EMPLOYER	37. DATES OF LAST EMPL'MT.	38. MAIN CIVILIAN OCCUPATION AND D. O. T. NO.
School	FROM None TO	Student 000.000

39. JOB PREFERENCE (LIST TYPE, LOCALITY, AND GENERAL AREA)	40. PREFERENCE FOR ADDITIONAL TRAINING (TYPE OF TRAINING)
School	Journalism, College
	44. VOCATIONAL OR TRADE COURSES (NATURE AND LENGTH OF COURSE)
	None

41. NON-SERVICE EDU. (YRS. SUCCESSFULLY COMPLETED)	42. DEGREES	43. MAJOR COURSE OR FIELD
GRAM. 8 H. S. 4 COL. 0	None	None

45. OFF DUTY EDUCATIONAL COURSES COMPLETED

None

47. DATE OF SEPARATION	46. SIGNATURE OF PERSON BEING SEPARATED
3-16-46	*Robert Bullard Perham*

A true copy of original VETERAN DISCHARGE recorded in this office on ___ 20, 1946.

ROBERT J. FIELD, Clerk.

= 247 =

C2607428   Series C

Honorable Discharge

from the

United States Navy

This is to certify that

Robert Bullard PERHAM   Fireman First Class, USNR

is **Honorably Discharged** *from the* U. S. NAVAL PERSONNEL SEPARATION CENTER
U. S. N. B. T. L. SAN PEDRO, CALIFORNIA

and from the Naval Service of the United States

this 16th *day of* March 1946

This certificate is awarded as a Testimonial of Fidelity and Obedience.

W. L. BOTTENBERG
LIEUT. (S) USNR
DISCHAR'E OFFICER
BY DIRECTION OF THE
COMMANDING OFFICER

Epilogue

_ _ _ _ _ _ _ _ _ _ _ _ _ _ _ _ _ _

Since that day, March 20, 1946, when I arrived at my grandmothers house in Greenwich Village, my life seems to have been, in retrospect, a series of adventures. Perhaps not the Richard Halliburton kind, but adventures nonetheless.

The first thing I did was to hitch-hike down to Clarksville, Georgia, where I became the only veteran in a community of 31 Quaker and Mennonite families. My girlfriend at the time was Joyce Rowland and she had a brother, Brad, who had been a conscientious objector from WWII. I had never heard that expression before that time, and was amazed to find out that some people actually refused to go to war. I was immediately attracted to the idea of meeting him and others like him. So I headed out, without telling Joyce or anyone else where I was going. I left town and started my new adventure.

I joined the community and befriended Brad who helped me get settled. He put me to work in the dairy barn where I was familiar with milking the cows (the milk was pasteurized, bottled and then donated to the local schools).

We had endless discussions around the kitchen table about the peace loving nature of their religion. I soon realized why they said no to war, and respected their integrity and their courage to endure humiliation of being treated like second class citizens.

Brad also had an extensive library. He got me reading again, mostly about various socialist writers of the time. Such as, Upton Sinclair, Lincoln Steffens and Eugene Debs. I was particularly impressed with a passage by Eugene Debs; "Years ago I recognized my kinship with all living beings, and made up my mind that I was not a bit better than the meanest on earth. I said then, and I say now, that while there is a lower class I am in it, while there is a criminal element, I am of it, and while there is a soul in prison, I am not free."

I learned a hell of a lot in the six months that I lived there. This new knowledge really clinched my hatred of all wars. I returned to Rye, New York a better man. I have carried that truth throughout my life.

I then set out for St. Lawrence University in upstate New York, to educate myself in journalism. I went on the veterans Bill of Rights, and interestingly enough, few, if any fellow students were aware that I was a veteran. Though not ashamed of having served, it just wasn't a topic that I liked to talk about.

After my sophomore year, I left school with the intention of taking a freighter to Peru. I was unable to join the seaman's union, so I hitch-hiked to California instead. After a year of working in California's first supermarket, Hirams' Ranch Market in Lynwood, a suburb of Los Angeles, I returned to St. Lawrence University where I graduated with honors. I had been the editor of the school literary magazine "The Laurentian", and had become a prolific writer.

I then married and started a family while living in New York. I had begun work at W.R. Grace & Company. I had a desk job and desperately wanted to get out of the country. So with my wife and three children, I transferred to Lima, Peru, where as head of the public relations department, I became involved in bullfighting (that's another story) and the wonderful world of theatre. I won the Tiahuanaco Award for my performance as "The Rain Maker" and I was hooked from then on. Stu Monroe, my good friend, was an expatriate, and living in Lima. He was the one who introduced me to bullfighting, and after he saw my performance in "Rain Maker", he convinced me to pursue acting.

After two years, we moved back to New York and took up residence in Scarsdale. I was still with W.R. Grace and had become their speech writer. Two nights a week I studied acting at the Eli Rill Studio in New York City. Among my classmates was an apparently awkward sixteen year old girl with a determined demeanor. Her name was Barbara Streisand.

During my lunch hours, I would audition for commercials and search for an agent. I wound up with four different television commercials which aired at the same time, affording me the opportunity to leave W.R. Grace in June of 1958. In October of that year, Eli Rill announced in class that there was a Broadway audition for "Look Homeward Angel". I auditioned and got a part alongside Mariam Hopkins and Ed Begley.

After closing on Broadway, we went on tour to Philadelphia and the "Coconut Grove" in Florida. After the play closed, I went home and told my wife that I had changed my name to Jeremy Slate and that I was moving to California to pursue my acting career. By that time we had four children, Jefre, Jamie, Jeremy, and Jason. My plan was to move them out to California when I became established.

I soon found work in Los Angeles, playing bit parts in popular television shows. I was introduced to Ivan Tors, the producer of "Sea Hunt". It wasn't long before I had my own series, "The Aquanauts/Malibu Run". It had been six months and I was now ready to send for my family.

I had many adventures throughout the next decade, participating in both television and feature films. I was lucky enough to work alongside many of the greats like John Wayne, Bob Hope, William Holden, Elvis Presley, Dennis Hopper and many more very talented actors.

In 1961, I joined the Hollywood Hackers, a professional golf group consisting of mostly working actors and some directors and writers. We played a tournament every week-end and sometimes my foursome included such luminaries as Larry Fine and John Agar.

One particular tournament was held on Catalina Island. As a publicity tie-in, Volkswagon was promoting their Aqua Car, a tiny half Volkswagon half Renault, that had been built to be driven on land and on water. In seven Aqua Cars the Hollywood Hackers drove twenty six miles across the sea from Newport Beach to Avalon. We traveled at a knot and a half, making the one way trip in six or so hours. What a ride! By the time we had reached Catalina, most of the cars had taken on water due to the extra passengers and we were a sorry sight arriving at Avalon. But, we made it and played the tournament.

The cars were garaged and not expected to take the trip back to Newport Beach. The next afternoon, Sunday, I found one of them in a garage and asked the mechanic when the car would be ready to go. No one else dared to take the trip back...except me, the adventurer. The mechanic said that the car could roll at any time. I had a few drinks and contemplated my trip, and when I got up to leave, a man who had missed out on the trip over suggested that he be my co-pilot that evening. His name was Jack and he was a speech writer for one of the Kennedys.

We set out just about midnight. We had to sneak out of Avalon harbor because small craft warnings were up. We cruised from boat to boat with our headlights out until we cleared the harbor. At that time, we saw three distant lights. We decided that we should head for the middle one, it probably being San Pedro. When we were far enough away from the harbor, we turned our headlights on. The sight was awesome: in heavy ground swells, as the hood dipped under the water, and the ocean came up to the windshield, the headlights revealed armies of fish swimming across our bow and obviously attracted by the lights. We were both fascinated, and unafraid. Especially me, as I had my set of fins on board. Neither of us was wearing a life jacket. Seven and a half hours later we drove into San Pedro harbor and right up onto the beach. The Coast Guard watched in amazement, knowing where we had come from. I therefore became the only person that I know of who has driven round trip to Catalina Island. That was both a caper and an adventure.

At this time, I also became a songwriter. I wrote" Just Beyond The Moon", and my friend Dorsey Burnette got the song to Tex Ritter. Tex recorded it and it became a hit. Thank you Dorsey. I remember the first time that I heard it on the car radio. I was driving along and the song came on. It was just surreal enough to make me pull over to the side of the road.

I also wrote a song called, "Every Time I Itch". Dennis Hopper heard it when we were filming "True Grit" and suggested to Glen Campbell that he record it. Glen changed the music and put the song on the flip side of his hit, "Galveston" which ended up selling over a million copies. Thank you Dennis, thank you Glen.

At this time, I walked out on my wife Beverly and my four beautiful children which triggered an ugly divorce. It was one of the few bad adventures in my life, something I have regretted ever since.

Two years later I met and married Tammy Grimes. Tammy was (and still is) a Broadway star whose true home was New York City. It was also her true love; after two years of marriage, we divorced and she went back to New York and I stayed out in Los Angeles.

After ten years, I grew tired of life in L.A....and the auditions...and dropped out (as my friend Timothy Leary put it). I found myself nude at Sandstone in Topanga Canyon trying to find a new direction. It was there that I met an anthropologist named Sally Binford. I also met Daniel Ellsberg and Anthony J. Russo. They confided in Sally and me that they were getting ready to release the Pentagon Papers which later became the essential tool in ending the Vietnam war and Nixons' reign. We once hid them out in our house in Venice; in retrospect it's weird to know that in the trunk of their car, were documents powerful enough to change the world as we saw it.

The next six years were spent on the road. Sally and I traveled around the United States, including Hawaii,

Canada, and Mexico in our motor home searching for peace and freedom. We became involved in many anti-war demonstrations and we were staunch supporters in the Womens' movement. It was at this time that I became a father once again. Another daughter, Reba, was born to a dear friend in Big Sur who insisted on being a single mother.

In 1980, I found myself needing to go back to work. I landed a good job in New York working on "One Life To Live", a popular Soap Opera, as Chuck Wilson. After five exciting years, I returned to California to be closer to my kids after finding out that my eldest son, Jefre, was striken with HIV. That news changed everything. I no longer wanted to act. I just wanted to be a good father.

Ten years later, when Jef and I were living together in Pacific Grove, he died at the age of forty four after living a wonderful life in the Redwood forests of Big Sur, on the property which I purchased in 1970. He was a brilliant musician and prophet. He touched many lives with his talent. I now live in the cabin that he once lived in, and I feel his presence everyday.

Six years ago, I met my future wife Denise Mellinger at a cocktail party at the Monterey Film Commission. Not only did we have film in common but she was also a writer. An added treat was that she was a Big Sur woman and didn't mind living in the woods. Actually she loves it.

Living here on the family property, (I gave the property to my kids as equal partners) amongst my kids and grandkids. I am finally living the adventure of my lifetime. I am a grandpa and a writer. And like Richard Halliburton, I have so many experiences to record. I have become a teacher, so to speak, of the past...the way it was, and I am so thankful for my opportunities.

On the morning of 9-11-01, Denise and I were in Larchmont, eighteen miles from New York City, waiting for our limousine to JFK for a return flight to California. Needless to say, we extended our visit and witnessed some powerful scenes. We couldn't see the devastation of Manhatten, but we did witness the devastation of the bedroom communities. The emptied firehouses and families left waiting for their people to come home.

On the scary flight home to California, we decided to drop out and follow our bliss. Denise is a prolific writer, and losing my eyesight to Macular Degeneration, we work together as a writing team here in the lovely Redwoods of Big Sur.

My three years in the Navy treated me to a wealth of information that I've used throughout my life. My experience in Clarksville, among the Quakers and the Mennonites, primed me to become a Lennonite; I have always felt close to John Lennon and Yoko Ono and preach their words every chance possible. Denise and I respect Johns prophecy and truly believe it could change the world...Imagine.

At the end of WWII, I thought the war was over for

good. When the United States became involved in the Korean war I was appalled to think that we were stupid enough to involve ourselves in another war. By the time Vietnam happened I was disgusted with the whole waste. Remembering our parade when we came home from war, I felt particularly bad for the Vietnam vets coming home to spit wads and 'fuck you's'. What a contrast to my experience!

There are two items that concern me deeply at this writing; one, the free use of the word 'kill' by our leaders. That has never been allowed in the history of our country. Second, the outright invasion of another country without proper provocation. (Vietnam veterans will remember the Gulf of Tionkin; we were lied to. There never was an invasion in the Gulf of Tionkin, but it was created in order to send our troops to Vietnam.) It appears that this administration doesn't even bother to come up with a lie.

Now I've lived for more than three quarters of a century, and I have witnessed many changes, I fear for the future of my grandchildren and the future condition of society. If such basic laws are ignored or tampered with, the structure of our great country will weaken and collapse. Take heed! God Speed!

Denise and Jeremy.

Made in the USA
San Bernardino, CA
14 February 2017